Socket.IO Real-time Web Application Development

Build modern real-time web applications powered by Socket.IO

Rohit Rai

BIRMINGHAM - MUMBAI

Socket.IO Real-time Web Application Development

First published: February 2013

Production Reference: 1120213

Published by Packt Publishing Ltd.
Livery Place
35 Livery Street
Birmingham B3 2PB, UK..

ISBN 978-1-78216-078-6

www.packtpub.com

Cover Image by Suresh Mogre (suresh.mogre.99@gmail.com)

Credits

Author
Rohit Rai

Reviewers
Arnout Kazemier
Andrew Keig

Acquisition Editor
Wilson D'souza

Commisioning Editor
Harsha Bharwani

Technical Editors
Ishita Malhi
Dominic Pereira

Copy Editors
Aditya Nair
Alfida Paiva
Ruta Waghmare

Project Coordinator
Esha Thakker

Proofreader
Elinor Perry Smith

Indexer
Rekha Nair

Graphics
Valentina D'Silva

Production Coordinator
Nilesh R. Mohite

Cover Work
Nilesh R. Mohite

About the Author

Rohit Rai is an accomplished software engineering professional and entrepreneur with several years of experience in developing products and consulting with clients on a variety of technologies, from enterprise applications on .NET and Java EE, consumer web applications focusing on JavaScript, data engineering and analytics platforms such as Pentaho and Hadoop, to modern platforms such as Groovy, Scala, and Node.js.

He is a founder of TupleJump, a startup building a new-generation data engineering platform for unifying and optimizing the workflows of data scientists, engineers, and analysts, bringing in innovative data process development approaches and modern visualization frameworks, all built on cutting-edge technologies designed to scale transparently from a single machine to large, distributed big data clusters.

He has previously worked with Cordys R&D, Pramati technologies, and various startups. He has consulted with clients like Intel and Sun, helping them develop products like Mash Maker and Zembly, powered by JavaScript. He was a member of one of the first teams on SocialTwist and developed one of the first widgets as a service platform and framework, which continues to power this widely-successful social media marketing and referral platform used by many Fortune 500 companies.

In open source, Rohit is a core committer and the administrator of Matisse (`http://www.matisse.org/`), the collaborative design platform. He is also the creator of socket.io.play, the Socket.IO module for the Play framework, and various open source projects hosted at GitHub (`https://github.com/rohit-tingendab`).

Acknowledgement

Writing a book, especially your first one, is an uphill and demanding task that cannot be accomplished by a single person without support from several others, and this book is no different. I would like to thank everyone who has played a role in helping me write this book or helping me reach the point where I could think of writing my own book. Though I cannot mention all the people by name, I am heartily grateful and indebted to everyone. However, I would like to mention the people who have played a directly important role in this book.

First of all, I have to thank my father and his elder brother, my uncle, who together, played the most important role in my personal and academic development. They inscribed on my mind, the importance of learning and knowledge above all else in life.

I would like to thank my wife, Paridhi, and my brother, Rajat, for bearing with my tantrums and idiosyncrasies, and still understanding and supporting me during my long hours of work and writing. I couldn't have pulled it off without them. The other very important person that I need to mention is my cousin, Shiti, who was always reviewing the book, giving exceptional feedback, running, debugging, and correcting the code for me, and also taking over quite a bit of my workload and my projects whenever she could. I have to thanks all my friends and cousins who played an important role in my upbringing, and who understood my missing all their parties and celebrations all the time.

I have to thank my friends, partners, and founders at my two ventures, Satyaprakash at TupleJump and Guillermo at Happymer, who have unconditionally supported me through the writing of this book and coped with me missing meetings and running slow at work from time to time.

I thank Pramati Technologies, the place where I learned most of what I know today and spent most of my career. I thank Jay and Vijay Pullur for starting this wonderful company; it is one of the very best places to work at.

I have to thank my managers, mentors, and guides at Pramati, specially Ramesh Loganathan, Chandrasekhar Sivaram, and KVP who have taught me a lot. All of them helped develop particular skill sets within me, without which I could never have written a book or started my own company. Chandru and KVP gave me the freedom to choose my projects, run my teams my way, and also the support to build Matisse and socket.io.play. Ramesh, who was the first published author I got to know in person, is my inspiration to write. Talking about mentors, I owe my professional success to Vivek Lakshman, my manager at Cordys and SocialTwist, my mentor, protector, guide, and above all, a friend I probably didn't do much to deserve. He has always challenged me to set higher goals for myself and then supported and pushed me to achieve these targets. The positive energy that he brings to any conversation helps boost the morale of everyone around.

My thanks go to everyone at Pramati for helping me, assisting me, and guiding me from time to time. I must thank my friends and colleagues, Apurba and Sunny (now at Sprinklr), who have always challenged me to learn more, explore more, and keep improving from time to time. Sunny was the one who forced me to dig deeper in JavaScript and functional programming during our SocialTwist days. And Apurba is someone from whom I have learned a lot; I still feel like a student in his presence.

The acknowledgements for a book on any technology would be incomplete without thanking the creators. I am thankful to Ryan Dahl, the creator of Node.js and Guillermo Rauch, the creator of socket.io, and the countless open source contributors to these and other enabling technologies, without whom these projects, and in turn this book, would have been impossible.

Last but not the least, I have to thank the team of editors and reviewers for this book. I thank the editors at Packt, Manali, Harsha, and Esha, who have been very good to me, understood the challenges for a first-time writer, and been considerate with delays and shuffling of deadlines. I also thank the reviewers who have done an excellent job of pointing out what is missing in the book, correcting the mistakes, and reviewing the code. Thank you guys, you have been great!

About the Reviewers

Arnout Kazemier is a Software Engineer from the Netherlands. He was originally schooled as a multimedia designer, but quickly rolled in to the world of frontend development and started to appreciate the beauty of JavaScript. After finding out that it was also possible to write JavaScript on the server side, he started using Aptana Jaxer and Narwal in his spare time. It wasn't until much later that Arnout heard about Node.js and its possibilities, and decided to take it for a spin when version 0.1.3 was released. Since then, he has never looked back. When Arnout joined the first Node.js hackatron (Node Knockout 2010), he built a real-time heat mapping engine on Node.js using Socket.IO. During the programming contest he learned a lot about Socket.IO and solved tons of issues that he encountered during the development of his entry. When the contest ended, he didn't stop contributing to Socket.IO, eventually becoming the first core team member of Socket.IO. He has been talking at different tech conferences since. Fast forwarding to 2013, he now spends time working on his own startup website `http://observe.it` (it won Node Knockout 2011) which allows you to observe and learn from your user's behavior in real time. He's still actively involved with the development of Socket.IO and conducts research on the connectivity of the real-time web and the impact of firewalls & virus scanners.

Andrew Keig has been building cutting-edge web applications for over 12 years. Andrew is a director at `airasoul.net`, which he runs with his artist wife Rima. Airasoul specializes in the design and build of scalable, RESTful, specification-driven, real-time web and mobile-based applications on both the Node.js and .NET stacks.

Andrew has a degree in Computing, and blogs at `blog.airasoul.net` on topics he is passionate about, such as Node.js, REST, Web APIs and Behavior-Driven Development. Andrew contributes to various open source projects for Node.js and .NET.

Andrew lives in London with his family: wife Rima and his son and inspiration, Indie.

www.PacktPub.com

Support files, eBooks, discount offers and more

You might want to visit www.PacktPub.com for support files and downloads related to your book.

Did you know that Packt offers eBook versions of every book published, with PDF and ePub files available? You can upgrade to the eBook version at www.PacktPub.com and as a print book customer, you are entitled to a discount on the eBook copy. Get in touch with us at service@packtpub.com for more details.

At www.PacktPub.com, you can also read a collection of free technical articles, sign up for a range of free newsletters and receive exclusive discounts and offers on Packt books and eBooks.

http://PacktLib.PacktPub.com

Do you need instant solutions to your IT questions? PacktLib is Packt's online digital book library. Here, you can access, read and search across Packt's entire library of books.

Why Subscribe?

- Fully searchable across every book published by Packt
- Copy and paste, print and bookmark content
- On demand and accessible via web browser

Free Access for Packt account holders

If you have an account with Packt at www.PacktPub.com, you can use this to access PacktLib today and view nine entirely free books. Simply use your login credentials for immediate access.

Table of Contents

Preface

Real-time web applications have traditionally been a challenging thing to achieve, relying on hacks and illusions. Many people avoid going real-time under the assumption of the complexity involved. This book will show you how to build modern, real-time web applications powered by Socket.IO, introducing you to various features of Socket.IO and walking you through the development, hosting, and scaling of a chat server.

What this book covers

Chapter1, Going Real Time on the Web, introduces us to the world of real-time web applications and their history.

Chapter 2, Getting Started with Node.js, introduces Node.js and its friends. Node.js is the platform that empowers many modern web applications, which are all written in JavaScript.

Chapter3, Let's Chat, gets us up and running with our first single-page chat system, introducing us to the Socket.IO API for real-time communication.

Chapter4, Making It More Fun!, adds more features to our chat application, such as giving our users a name, having multiple chat rooms, and integrating express with Socket.IO sessions.

Chapter5, The Socket.IO Protocol, explains the Socket.IO protocol, its mechanism and working.

Chapter6, Deploying and Scaling, explains the intricacies involved in taking our chat system to production and scaling it out.

Appendix A, Socket.IO Quick Reference, is a reference for the Socket.IO API.

Appendix B, Socket.IO Backends, lists a few alternative backend implementations for different languages and platforms.

What you need for this book

To use this book, we don't presume any special requirements in software. You will need a PC with Linux or Windows OS or a Mac. You can use any text editor for coding, but having a programmer's editor such as Vi, Emacs, Notepad++, Sublime Text, or any IDE of your choice will help. We will be installing the remaining software, such as Node.js and npm, as we go through the book and when they are required.

Who this book is for

This book is aimed at developers who want to start developing highly interactive and real-time web applications such as chat systems, online multiplayer games, or want to introduce real-time updates or server push mechanisms in their existing applications. Knowledge of developing in JavaScript and web applications in general is expected. Though there is a chapter on introducing Node.js, prior knowledge of Node.js will be a plus. Readers will need access to a computer system capable of running Node.js, a test or code editor, and access to the Internet to download the required software and components.

Conventions

In this book, you will find a number of styles of text that distinguish between different kinds of information. Here are some examples of these styles, and an explanation of their meaning.

Code words in text are shown as follows: "To set the environment our node server runs in, we set an environment variable NODE_ENV to the environment we want to run node in."

A block of code is set as follows:

```
<!DOCTYPE html>
<html>
<head>
<title>{TITLE}</title>
<link rel="stylesheet" href="/stylesheets/style.css" />
</head>
```

```
<body>
<header id="banner">
<h1>Awesome Chat</h1>
</header>
     {CONTENT}
<footer>
       Hope you enjoy your stay here
</footer>
</body>
</html>
```

When we wish to draw your attention to a particular part of a code block, the relevant lines or items are set in bold:

```
doctype 5
html
   block head
      title= title
      link(rel='stylesheet', href='/stylesheets/style.css')
   body
header#banner
h1 Awesome Chat
      block content
      footer Hope you enjoy your stay here
```

Any command-line input or output is written as follows:

```
$ express awesome-chat
$ cd awesome-chat
$ npm install
```

New terms and **important words** are shown in bold. Words that you see on the screen, in menus or dialog boxes for example, appear in the text like this: "Now you can enter your message in the message box in one of the browsers and click **Send**. You will see it appear on the message area of both the browsers."

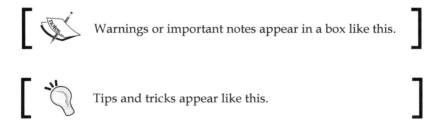

Warnings or important notes appear in a box like this.

Tips and tricks appear like this.

Reader feedback

Feedback from our readers is always welcome. Let us know what you think about this book—what you liked or may have disliked. Reader feedback is important for us to develop titles that you really get the most out of.

To send us general feedback, simply send an e-mail to feedback@packtpub.com, and mention the book title via the subject of your message.

If there is a topic that you have expertise in and you are interested in either writing or contributing to a book, see our author guide on www.packtpub.com/authors.

Customer support

Now that you are the proud owner of a Packt book, we have a number of things to help you to get the most from your purchase.

Downloading the example code

You can download the example code files for all Packt books you have purchased from your account at http://www.packtpub.com. If you purchased this book elsewhere, you can visit http://www.packtpub.com/support and register to have the files e-mailed directly to you.

Errata

Although we have taken every care to ensure the accuracy of our content, mistakes do happen. If you find a mistake in one of our books—maybe a mistake in the text or the code—we would be grateful if you would report this to us. By doing so, you can save other readers from frustration and help us improve subsequent versions of this book. If you find any errata, please report them by visiting http://www.packtpub.com/submit-errata, selecting your book, clicking on the **errata submission form** link, and entering the details of your errata. Once your errata are verified, your submission will be accepted and the errata will be uploaded on our website, or added to any list of existing errata, under the Errata section of that title. Any existing errata can be viewed by selecting your title from http://www.packtpub.com/support.

Piracy

Piracy of copyright material on the Internet is an ongoing problem across all media. At Packt, we take the protection of our copyright and licenses very seriously. If you come across any illegal copies of our works, in any form, on the Internet, please provide us with the location address or website name immediately so that we can pursue a remedy.

Please contact us at copyright@packtpub.com with a link to the suspected pirated material.

We appreciate your help in protecting our authors, and our ability to bring you valuable content.

Questions

You can contact us at questions@packtpub.com if you are having a problem with any aspect of the book, and we will do our best to address it.

1
Going Real Time on the Web

The Arab Spring revolution was sparked and fuelled through social media sites like Facebook and Twitter. Over the next few days, social media went from being just a means of interacting with family and friends to a weapon that empowered the people and brought about a significant change in the world. Everyone noticed the power of the people and people noticed what social networks were capable of. At the heart of it all was the technology that made all this possible, the technology that removed all the barriers to communication and spread the word faster than wildfire. This is the power of real-time web!

What is real-time web?

On the Web, we have been habituated to sites and applications where we click on a link or a button, or change some input and perform some action, and it causes some change in the page. But if we leave our twitter page open for a while, we get alerts when we receive new tweets, even without performing any action (shown in the next screenshot). This is what we mean in general when we say "real-time web".

Real-time updates on Twitter

Wikipedia introduces real-time web in these words:

> *The real-time web is a set of technologies and practices that enable users to receive information as soon as it is published by its authors, rather than requiring that they or their software check a source periodically for updates.*

This "set of technologies" is one of the hottest trends on the Web. Over the next few pages, we will get familiar with these technologies and see their use in various applications.

A bit of history

To understand and fully appreciate any concept, it is important to know where it came from and how it evolved.

Real-time web is not a new thing; one of the first attempts at making web real-time was the usage of Java applets. Many will remember chatting in Yahoo! chat rooms or playing chess, way back in the late '90s. Then came Flash and ActiveX plugins. This was not only for "fun" (for the consumer section), but also for use in the enterprise market. I worked for a BPM (Business Process Management) company in the early stages of my career, where they had built an ActiveX plugin for powering their dashboards and updating process information in real time. So why is it important now? Because the way in which real-time functionality is implemented and the cost involved in doing so has changed. From being a fancy feature in an application, it has become a necessity—a user demand. From being a hacked-in or technically challenging piece of the application, it is on its way to becoming a ratified standard in the form of WebSockets and Server-Sent Events (SSE). How did we get from static web to here?

The Web (and web applications), as we all know, is built over the HTTP protocol. HTTP is a request-response system, where the client sends a request for information to the server and the server responds with the requested information. In most cases, this information is the HTML or related information, like XML or JSON, to be rendered by the browser. This HTTP browser-server interaction is shown in the following figure:

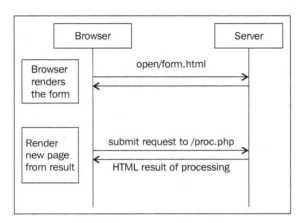

HTTP browser-server interaction

In 1995, Sun and Netscape announced a partnership that saw Netscape bundle Sun's brand new Java runtime with its browser. This was the beginning of highly interactive web. Although they have since earned themselves a very bad reputation, applets were the pioneers in the field of real-time web. In the early days of real-time web, we saw applets being used everywhere, for chat, games, and even for banners.

In the same year, Netscape came up with a scripting language called JavaScript (originally LiveScript), and another small company called FutureWave Software started working on an animation software called FutureSplash Animator. Later, both of them became the cause of Java applets almost disappearing from the Web.

FutureWave was acquired by Macromedia in 1996 and they renamed FutureSplash Animator to Flash. Flash, as we all know, went on to rule the Web as the most widely available platform for creating animations, games, video players, and everything interactive, for the major part of the next decade.

In 1999, Microsoft used its iframe technology and JavaScript to update news and stock quotes on Internet Explorer's default home page (`http://home.microsoft.com`). In the same year, they released a proprietary ActiveX extension for IE, called XMLHTTP. This was the era when XML was the "in" thing and everyone wanted to use XML for anything they were doing. This XMLHTTP component was originally meant to load XML data in the page asynchronously, using JavaScript. It was soon adopted by Mozilla, Safari, and Opera, as XMLHttpRequest (or XHR, for short). But it was with the launch of Gmail (by Google) that the term AJAX (Asynchronous JavaScript and XML)—coined by Jesse James Garrett in an article titled *Ajax: A New Approach to Web Applications*—became the buzzword in web development. The following figure shows an AJAX Request:

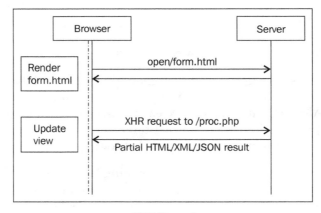

AJAX Request

Gmail also shed light on the advantages of live updates to web pages and opened the floodgates to various hacks built over AJAX to push data from a server (or at least, giving the illusion of doing so).

Collectively, these technologies were referred to as Comet-a term introduced by Alex Russell on his blog in 2006. Comet was a play on the word Ajax, both being popular household cleaners in the US. Comet was not one single approach. It introduced multiple mechanisms to give the feeling of data being pushed from the server to the client. These included Hidden iframe, XHR polling, XHR long polling, and Script tag long polling (or, JSONP long polling).

Let us understand how these work, as they continue to remain the most commonly available mechanisms across all modern browsers.

The first and the easiest to implement is XHR polling, in which the browser keeps polling for data periodically, and the server keeps responding with an empty response unless it has data to send back to the browser. Following an event, such as receiving a mail, or creating/updating a record in the database, the server responds to the next polling request with new data. The following figure depicts this mechanism:

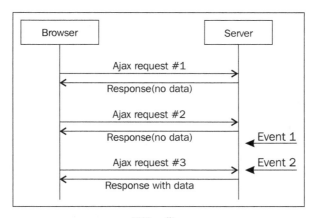

XHR polling

As you can see, there is a problem with this. The browser has to keep making requests to the server even when there is no data. This causes the server to get and process data even when there is nothing to deliver.

One of the solutions to this is to modify the server to piggyback the actual client requests by not only sending the data requested by the client, but also appending additional data that the server has, to send to the browser. The client needs to be modified to understand and act upon the additional incoming data. The HTTP piggybacking process is shown in the following figure:

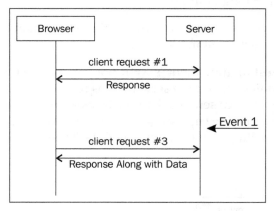

HTTP piggybacking

As the new data is only sent when there is a client action, it causes delays in the data reaching the browser. The solution to receiving events quickly while avoiding frequent server queries is long polling.

In long polling, when the browser sends a request to the server, the server won't respond immediately if it doesn't have data to respond with, and will suspend the request. Once the event occurs, the server closes the suspended request by sending over a response to the client. As soon as the client receives the response, it sends a new request:

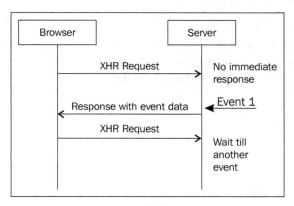

Long Polling

There are various ways in which long polling is implemented, such as forever iframe, multipart XHR, script tags with JSONP, and long-living XHR.

Though all these techniques work, these are hacks, bending HTTP and XHR to be able to do duplex communication, which is not what they are meant for.

With the rapid evolution of the web browsers lead by Firefox and then Chrome, the long-due upgrade to HTML, called HTML5, is being widely adopted. In HTML5, there are two new methods for pushing data from the server to the client. One is Server-Sent Events (SSE) and the other is the full duplex WebSockets.

Server-Sent Events attempts to standardize Comet-like communication across browsers. In this approach, there is a JavaScript API to create an event source, that is, a stream over which the server can send events. This is a unidirectional protocol. We will still be using the good old XHR. This is a good approach when you don't need full duplex communication; just push updates from the server to client.

The other specification which goes on to implement a full duplex communication protocol for the web applications is WebSockets. In WebSockets, the client initiates a socket connection with the server, which supports this protocol as well. The server and client will send and receive data on this socket connection.

Applications of real-time web

Let us take a quick look at how real-time web is changing the applications we come across on the Web daily.

Gaming

With the success of Zynga and other social gaming companies, online gaming has become a hot trend. WordSquared is a massively parallel online multiplayer crossword, while BrowserQuest is an attempt (by Mozilla) at building an in-browser real-time role-playing game. One of the more popular and publicized games built on socket.io is Rawkets. There are many open source game engines built over canvas and around real-time communication systems.

Social stream updates

Twitter is the best example of getting real-time data (the tweets) to the browser without user action. Google+ and Facebook have it too. The important thing on social networks is, being updated about happenings in real time.

Business applications

CRMs are some of the most important components in business acquisitions. The days of issue tracking systems being sold as CRMs are over. CRMs are continuously improving and re-inventing themselves. Most of the CRMs are adding social capabilities; they are adding more functionality everyday. Salesforce, one of the most popular hosted CRM solutions, introduced Chatter. Chatter adds social capabilities to CRM and brings in a lot of advantages powered by realtime updates. It allows the customers to add comments or post updates on issues, which appear in real time to the support associates on their system. BPM solutions are also integrating real-time components to keep a track on process status and updates.

Web-based monitors

The latest updates to Google Analytics include a functionality to see the real-time updates of users visiting your website. Splunk — an event-tracking system, which is widely used to monitor events on infrastructure and machine data — allows you monitor and track event updates on the charts, updated in real time.

Summary

In the chapter, we saw what real-time web looks like, what its applications are, and how the technologies around real-time web evolved over a decade of development. In the next chapter we will get acquainted with Node.js, the JavaScript web application development platform which is the primary target of socket.io.

2
Getting Started with Node.js

The definition of Node.js that is given on the Node.js website
(http://nodejs.org/), is as follows:

> *Node.js is a platform built on Chrome's JavaScript runtime for easily building*
> *fast, scalable network applications. Node.js uses an event-driven, non-blocking I/O*
> *model that makes it lightweight and efficient, perfect for data-intensive real-time*
> *applications that run across distributed devices.*

What matters to us is, Node.js as a part of the platform, provides a scalable and
high-performance web application development framework, which allows
programming in JavaScript.

Many of us got introduced to JavaScript while building websites or web applications
for DOM manipulation, AJAX, and related stuff. But JavaScript is much more
than that. Just like C, Java, Python, and so on, JavaScript is also a full-fledged
programming language. In all browsers, JavaScript is executed in a virtual
machine (VM), in the context of the browser. But it can also be executed in
another context—as in the case of a Node.js backend—without the browser.

Node.js uses Google Chrome's JavaScript VM to execute JavaScript applications
outside the browser, on the server. Along with this runtime environment,
Node.js also provides a library of modules, which provides a framework for
building network applications. Node.js is not a web server like the Apache HTTP
server, or an application server like Tomcat; but as part of its modules library,
Node.js does provide an HTTP Server, which can be used to build web applications.

Apart from having JavaScript as the programming language for the applications,
one thing that sets Node.js (and most of the Node.js modules and applications)
apart from the traditional servers and applications is the asynchronous event-driven
development model, which we will see in later sections.

The origin of Node.js

This is not the first time that JavaScript has been used for server-side programming. Netscape launched Netscape Enterprise Server in 1996, which allowed server-side programming in JavaScript. Since then, many servers, such as **RingoJS** (http://ringojs.org/), **Persevere** (http://www.persvr.org/), Mozilla's Rhino-based servers, and others have tried to follow suit.

A major reason for these servers not being taken seriously was the pitiful performance of the JavaScript VMs used by them. JavaScript performance in browsers was also not very good. That was until Google launched its Chrome web browser.

At the time of its launch, Chrome's JavaScript VM, called **V8**, was almost 10-20 times faster than any other JavaScript VM, and has since then been the fastest.

It was based on this VM that Ryan Dahl developed Node.js in 2008. He wanted to build a server that would enable and empower real-time interactive web applications like Gmail. But Node.js was not the first server he built. Ryan built Ebb, a web server based on Ruby and C, but realized that it wasn't working as fast as he wanted it to. This was followed by several experiments in building a number of small web servers.

Armed with the knowledge gained from his experiments and the study of various platforms, he decided to develop an event-driven or asynchronous server. In the January of 2008, he came up with the idea of building a small web server based on JavaScript. He was inclined towards JavaScript because it was independent of the OS and came without any I/O APIs. He quit his job and worked on Node.js for 6 months. In November 2009, he presented Node.js in JSConf, and has been working for Joyent since then. Initially, Node.js worked only on Unix-based systems; later, it came with support for Windows OS too.

Why Node.js

Node.js is a new platform and is still evolving (not even a version 1.0 has been released yet), but even in its infancy, it is probably one of the most popular platforms on the Web. It is already powering a large number of popular services. Let us take a look at what makes Node.js such a tempting and popular proposition.

JavaScript everywhere

The first and foremost advantage of Node.js is JavaScript. If you know and code in JavaScript regularly, you already know most of Node.js; all that's left to learn can be thought of as APIs and best practices.

Node.js — built over Google Chrome's V8 JavaScript engine — allows entire applications to be written using JavaScript. We have already been writing frontends in JavaScript; with Node.js, we write the backend as well, in the same language that we have honed our skills on and grown to love. It saves every frontend developer from learning one more language or relying on some other developer to expose the RESTful APIs required by their application.

Event-driven design

Node.js was designed around events and callbacks. As a JavaScript developer, you would already be familiar with the concept of listening to events and using callbacks. Node.js incorporates this philosophy in each and every aspect of the platform. Be it in server request handling, I/O, or database interactions, everything in Node.js will ideally be handled by a callback attached to an event by a listener.

This brings us to one of the most important concepts behind Node.js, that is, the *event loop*. I like the fast food restaurant analogy by Dan York (http://code.danyork.com) for explaining event loop-based systems.

Consider a restaurant where you go to the cashier, place your order, and wait till your food is ready. In this case, the cashier cannot serve the other customers till you have your order, and the queue is blocked. If the restaurant has a large inflow of customers and needs to scale up, they will have to invest in hiring more number of cashiers, creating more cash counters, and so on. This is similar to the traditional multithreading model.

In contrast, let us see the model many other restaurants use. In this case, you go to the cashier and place your order (which he/she hands over to the kitchen); he/she then accepts your payment and gives you a token. You then step aside, and the cashier moves on to the next customer. When your order is ready, the kitchen server announces this by calling your name or flashing your token number, and you walk up and fetch your order. This event-oriented approach optimizes the work of the cashier and lets you wait on the side, freeing up the relevant resources to service others until your work is done.

In Node.js, the server is the cashier, and all the handlers are the kitchen crew. The server accepts a request and spins it off to a handler. It then moves on to accept other requests. When the request is processed and the results are in place, the response is queued on the server and sent back to the client when it reaches the front of the queue.

As opposed to the traditional approach of launching the threads or processes of the server (which is similar to adding more cashiers), this method is more efficient, as the workers launched have dedicated responsibilities. This is much lighter and cheaper than replicating the entire server.

In the sections ahead, we will see that we register the handlers or the workers with the server to handle certain requests, and all the server does is delegate the requests to these workers.

The advantage of the event-driven design is that everything we design is non-blocking. "You don't wait on me, I call you" is the mantra that relieves us from the pain involved in waiting on a request to be fulfilled. It frees up the system resources that would have otherwise been spent in waiting on the request, so that they can be used for the other tasks in the queue. This allows the Node.js applications to give a very high performance and capability of handling a very high load.

Node.js is a modular framework with a modern module system from the ground up. Everything in Node.js is built as modules running in the V8 JavaScript engine. Every functionality in the platform is provided by means of modules. This keeps the platform lean and brings in only that what is required. Having a native module system also helps in keeping our applications modular.

JavaScript has become one of the most widely-used languages in the past few years and has a vibrant community. Node.js provides developers with a good platform that assists them in developing end-to-end applications in JavaScript. Node.js has also brought in many revolutionary concepts, namely, always asynchronous, non-blocking I/O, event-oriented servers, and so on. This has resulted in a very vibrant, large, and active community. New modules are coming up continuously, and the community provides active support and is very helpful. Most of the popular modules and frameworks built for Node.js generally come from the community and are mostly open source.

Corporate backing

Many companies have invested heavily in Node.js in the past couple of years. From Ryan Dahl's employer, Joyent, to the creators of the Mojito framework (Internet giant Yahoo!), many companies have built products, platforms, frameworks, and services around Node.js. This kind of corporate commitment assures a stable future.

How to get Node.js

Due to the popularity of Node.js, it is very easy to get it working on any operating system. You can go to `http://nodejs.org/` and download the appropriate distribution for your operating system.

 Though Node.js works on any OS, as it comes from the *nix background, many modules might only work on Linux or other Unix systems; so it is best to use such a system if you have one at hand.

If you are using Linux, in most cases, you should be able to install Node.js using your distribution's package manager. As this information keeps changing, I'll just point out the location instead. You'll find the instructions for installing Node.js using package manager here:

```
https://github.com/joyent/node/wiki/Installing-Node.js-via-package-
manager
```

If you are using Mac OS or Windows, you should know that Node.js now provides an installer for these platforms, which is the recommended installation approach. You can also install using the source. Instead of repeating that process here, which is again subject to change, I'll suggest that you follow the official installation instructions on the Node.js wiki, on GitHub (`https://github.com/joyent/node/wiki/Installation`).

Node.js package manager (npm)

If you installed Node.js using the installer from the Node.js website, you will already have npm installed.

Also, if you followed the instructions to build from the source, you will probably have installed npm. If that is a yes, very good! If no, please do so now. For this, I recommend that you follow the instructions mentioned in the npm installation documentation (`https://github.com/isaacs/npm/`).

You can check if you have npm installed by typing the following command:

```
$ npm -v
```

This should display the version of npm installed.

For those who are wondering what npm is and why you would need a package manager for Node.js, npm is just what its name says; it provides an infrastructure in Node.js to distribute and manage packages. As I said earlier, Node.js is very modular. Node.js apps are built using many modules and third-party packages because npm provides an easy way of adding and managing third-party dependencies for our applications. We will see more on its use in a while.

Hello World with Node.js

Here, the obligatory Hello World example uses Node.js. Write the following line in a file called `helloworld.js` and save it:

```
console.log("Hello World");
```

And now to run it, execute the following command:

node helloworld.js

This should print **Hello World** on the console. All the JavaScript developers will immediately recognize that these are the steps we follow to print anything on the console while developing a web application.

What happens is that Node.js loads the JavaScript file in the JavaScript VM, provides an environment for its execution, and the VM interprets the script. When it gets `console.log`, it checks the environment for the console, which in this case is STDOUT, and writes **Hello World** to it.

But we are here to develop web applications, correct? So let's say hello to the Web!

Hello Web

Let us make a very simple web application that greets the user with a hello. Write the following code in a file, and name it `helloweb.js`:

```
var http = require("http");

http.createServer(function(request, response) {
  response.writeHead(200, {"Content-Type": "text/html"});
  response.write("<html>");
  response.write("<head><title>Node.js</title></head>");
  response.write("<body>Hello Web</body>");
  response.write("</html>");
  response.end();
}).listen(9999);
```

To run the previous piece of code, execute `helloweb.js` in Node.js:

node helloweb.js

And then open `http://localhost:9999/` in your browser. You should see a page saying **Hello Web**. There is a lot going on here! So let us walk through the code and understand what is going on.

The very first line of code introduces us to one of the fundamental building blocks of Node.js, the module system. Node.js has a very simple module system built on CommonJS. Those familiar with frontend development using RequireJS with **Asynchronous Module Definition (AMD)** will immediately relate to this. All the functionality in Node.js is built as modules and you need to import it in your code using `require`. Node.js has several modules compiled in a binary form, called core modules, HTTP being one of them. We can also create and include our own custom or third-party modules using `require`. In case of file modules, there is one-to-one mapping between a file and a module; so we write every module in its own file. We will see more on writing our own modules later.

```
var http = require("http");
```

With this statement, Node.js will load the core HTTP module, and it will be available in a variable called `http`. The next task is to create a server using the HTTP module. This is done using the `createServer` method from the module. The `createServer` method accepts `requestListener`.

```
http.createServer([requestListener]);
```

The `requestListener` is a function that handles the incoming requests. In our case, this function is passed *inline*. Just like JavaScript in a browser, Node.js also runs a single process and a single thread. This is different from the traditional application servers, which create a new thread or process to handle new requests. So to scale and handle multiple requests, Node.js uses asynchronous event handling. So every request that comes in triggers an event, which is then handled by the event handler asynchronously. This is the mechanism of the event loop explained in earlier sections.

```
http.createServer(function(request, response) {
    response.writeHead(200, {"Content-Type": "text/html"});
    response.write("<html>");
    response.write("<head><title>Node.js JS</title></head>");
    response.write("<body>Hello Web</body>");
    response.write("</html>");
    response.end();
});
```

Downloading the example code

You can download the example code files for all Packt books you have purchased from your account at http://www.packtpub.com. If you purchased this book elsewhere, you can visit http://www.packtpub.com/support and register to have the files e-mailed directly to you.

The way `createServer` works is similar to any event handler in JavaScript. The event in this case is receiving a request to serve. As we can see, `requestListener` takes two arguments, `request` and `response`. The `request` object is an instance of `http.ServerRequest`, and will have all the information about the request, such as URL, method, headers, and data.

The `response` object is an instance of `ServerResponse`, which implements a `WritableStream`. It exposes various methods to write the response to the client; the ones we are most interested in, for now, are `writeHead`, `write` and `end`. Let us first see `writeHead`:

```
response.writeHead(statusCode, [reasonPhrase], [headers]);
```

Here, `statusCode` is the HTTP response code, `reasonPhrase` is the optional human-readable response phrase, and `headers` is the object that has the headers, which are to be sent in the response. This function should be called only once, before calling `response.end`. If we call `response.write` or `response.end` before this, the implicit/mutable headers will be calculated and the following function will be called automatically:

```
response.writeHead(200, {"Content-Type": "text/html"});
```

In this call, we are setting the status code to `200`, that is, HTTP OK, and we are only setting the `Content-Type` header to `text/html`. The next method here is `response.write`, it's used to write the response content to the client. The call to this method is done as follows:

```
response.write(chunk, [encoding]);
```

In this call, `chunk` is the content to write and `encoding` is the content encoding to use. If the chunk is a string and the encoding is not specified, UTF-8 will be used by default.

```
response.write("<html>");
response.write("<head><title>Node.js JS</title></head>");
response.write("<body>Hello Web</body>");
response.write("</html>");
```

In the above code, the first time `write` is called, Node.js sends the response headers and the chunk of the body. But the `write` method can then be called multiple times. Node.js will assume that we are streaming data, and will keep sending the chunk whenever the calls are made. And the last call on the response is made to tell Node.js that we are done. This is just what `response.end` does.

```
response.end([data], [encoding]);
```

`response.end` signals to the server that all the response headers and body content have been sent and that the server should consider this message complete. We *must* call this method for every message.

```
response.end();
```

In our case, we call `response.end` without any of the optional arguments. If we do pass in the parameters, it is equivalent to calling `response.write` with the parameters, followed by `response.end`. I prefer keeping them separate, and hence, explicit.

Finally, we need to tell the HTTP server which port it should listen on. In this case, we tell it to listen on port 9999.

```
listen(9999);
```

Routing the requests

Almost any web application serves more than a single resource. So now we know how to serve content using an HTTP server; but how do we handle multiple resources? Routing is the name of the game. We need to understand the incoming request and map it to the appropriate request handler. This is a bit more complicated than the previous example, so we will build it step by step, improving it with every step.

To demonstrate the routing of requests, let us build a simple application that serves two resources at /start and /finish, displaying **Hello** and **Goodbye** respectively. To simplify the code, we will serve plain text. So before anything else, let's take a look at the code:

```
var http = require("http");
var url = require("url");

function onRequest(request, response) {
  var pathname = url.parse(request.url).pathname;
  console.log("Request for " + pathname + " received.");
  if(pathname === "/start"){
    response.writeHead(200, {"Content-Type": "text/plain"});
    response.write("Hello");
    response.end();
  }else if(pathname === "/finish"){
    response.writeHead(200, {"Content-Type": "text/plain"});
    response.write("Goodbye");
    response.end();
  }else{
```

```
        response.writeHead(404, {"Content-Type": "text/plain"});
        response.end("404 Not Found");
    }
}

http.createServer(onRequest).listen(9999);
console.log("Server has started.");
```

Save the previous code snippet in a file called `routing.js` and execute it as follows:

node routing.js

Now, when we access `http://localhost:9999/start`, we will see **Hello** in the browser. Similarly, when we access `http://localhost:9999/finish`, we will see a message saying **Goodbye**. If we try to access any other path, we will get an HTTP 404 or Not Found error. Let us now try and understand the new things we are introducing in this example.

The first thing that we need in order to route a request, is to parse the URL; for this we will introduce another inbuilt module called `url`. When a URL string is parsed using the `url` module, it returns an instance of the URL. In this case, we are interested in the pathname.

```
var pathname = url.parse(request.url).pathname;
```

In the previous line of code, we are passing the `url` string from the request, and parsing it using the `url` module, to get the `pathname`. The next step is to send an appropriate response, based on the path being accessed:

```
    if(pathname === "/start"){
      response.writeHead(200, {"Content-Type": "text/plain"});
      response.write("Hello");
      response.end();
    }else if(pathname === "/finish"){
      response.writeHead(200, {"Content-Type": "text/plain"});
      response.write("Goodbye");
      response.end();
    }
```

Here we are comparing the pathname with the one we are expected to handle, and accordingly an appropriate response is sent out. And what happens to the requests we don't handle? That is what the last part of the if-else-if ladder does. It sends an HTTP 404 error.

```
        response.writeHead(404, {"Content-Type": "text/plain"});
        response.end("404 Not Found");
```

Now let us think about extending this application. To handle more paths, we will have to add more if-else conditions. But that doesn't look clean, is difficult to read, and is very inefficient in execution. Think about the route handled in the last step of the if-else ladder; the process still has to go through the entire ladder, checking for every condition. Also, adding new routes to this will require us to go through and edit this if-else ladder, which will be at the very least, confusing, and can also easily result in errors, typos, and a high chance of unintentional modification to the existing routes. So let us make it a bit cleaner by putting the handlers in an object mapped by their paths, and also provide an API to extend it. So let us change our code to look like this:

```javascript
var http = require("http");
var url = require("url");

var route = {
  routes : {},
  for: function(path, handler){
    this.routes[path] = handler;
  }
};

  route.for("/start", function(request, response){
    response.writeHead(200, {"Content-Type": "text/plain"});
    response.write("Hello");
    response.end();
  });

  route.for("/finish", function(request, response){
    response.writeHead(200, {"Content-Type": "text/plain"});
    response.write("Goodbye");
    response.end();
  });

function onRequest(request, response) {
  var pathname = url.parse(request.url).pathname;
  console.log("Request for " + pathname + " received.");
  if(typeof route.routes[pathname] ==='function'){
    route.routes[pathname](request, response);
  }else{
    response.writeHead(404, {"Content-Type": "text/plain"});
    response.end("404 Not Found");
  }
}

http.createServer(onRequest).listen(9999);
console.log("Server has started.");
```

To run this code snippet, execute the file with Node.js, using the following command:

```
node resources.js
```

The functionality of the application will be the same as the result of the previous example. When we access either /start or /finish, it will respond with **Hello** for the former, and **Goodbye** for the latter. On trying to access any other path, we will get an HTTP 404 message.

The change we have made here is that we have thrown out the if-else-if ladder in favor of a clean and efficient design approach. In this approach, we don't need to play around with existing routes and can add new routes by calling the route.for method from any module. The route has a map of the path to the handler function and also has a on method to add new routes.

```
var route = {
  routes : {},
  for: function(path, handler){
    this.routes[path] = handler;
  }
}

route.on("/start", function(request, response){
    response.writeHead(200, {"Content-Type": "text/plain"});
    response.write("Hello");
    response.end();
});

route.on("/finish", function(request, response){
    response.writeHead(200, {"Content-Type": "text/plain"});
    response.write("Goodbye");
    response.end();
});
```

Here we are adding two new handlers for the paths /start and /finish. The signature for the handlers is similar to the main request handler. We expect the handlers to get the request and response, so that the handler has everything it needs to process the request and send the response.

```
if (typeof(route.routes[pathname])==='function')
```

In the if condition, we check whether the route for the pathname is present, and whether it is a function. If we find a handler for the requested path, we execute the handler function, passing the request and response to it.

```
route.routes[pathname](request, response);
```

If it is not found, we respond with an HTTP 404 error. Now, to add a new path, we can call the `route.on` method with the path and its handler to register it.

```
route.on("/newpath", function(request, response){
    response.writeHead(200, {"Content-Type": "text/plain"});
    response.write("new response");
    response.end();
});
```

HTTP Methods

HTTP is not only about the path, we also have to think about the HTTP methods. In this section, we will enhance our app to handle the different HTTP methods: GET, POST, PUT, and DELETE.

As the first step towards this, we will add the ability to add different handlers for different methods. We will add the methods in the mapping in resources.js, which is a minor change. This is shown in the following code snippet:

```
var http = require("http");
var url = require("url");
var route = {
  routes : {},
  for: function(method, path, handler){
    this.routes[method + path] = handler;
  }
}

  route.for("GET", "/start", function(request, response){
    response.writeHead(200, {"Content-Type": "text/plain"});
    response.write("Hello");
    response.end();
  });

  route.for("GET", "/finish", function(request, response){
    response.writeHead(200, {"Content-Type": "text/plain"});
    response.write("Goodbye");
    response.end();
  });

function onRequest(request, response) {
  var pathname = url.parse(request.url).pathname;
  console.log("Request for " + request.method + pathname +
  " received.");
```

```
      if(typeof(route.routes[request.method +
pathname])==='function'){
        route.routes[request.method + pathname](request, response);
      }else{
        response.writeHead(404, {"Content-Type": "text/plain"});
        response.end("404 Not Found");
      }
    }

    http.createServer(onRequest).listen(9999);
    console.log("Server has started.");
```

Save the file and execute with Node.js. The functionality still remains the same, but we will be able to handle different methods using different handlers. Let us create a new handler to echo the incoming data on POST.

```
    route.on("POST", "/echo", function(request, response){
      var incoming = "";
      request.on('data', function(chunk) {
        incoming += chunk.toString();
      });

      request.on('end', function(){
        response.writeHead(200, {"Content-Type": "text/plain"});
        response.write(incoming);
        response.end();
      });
    });
```

Here we are adding a new handler for the POST request on the /echo path. We again see the use of the event-driven approach of Node.js, this time in handling the data that comes in with POST. Since request is an event emitter, we attach an event handler to it for each task: for handling chunks of incoming data and for completing the request processing once all the data is received.

```
    request.on('data', function(chunk) {
      incoming += chunk.toString();
    });
```

In the previous piece of code, we add a listener on the request to handle chunks of incoming data. In this case, all we do is accumulate the incoming data.

```
    request.on('end', function(){
      response.writeHead(200, {"Content-Type": "text/plain"});
      response.write(incoming);
      response.end();
    });
```

The event handler on end will be invoked once all the data sent in POST has been received. This is the time at which we finish receiving all the data. To build an echo service, we will send back all the accumulated data. We will now create a form to post the request to this handler.

```
route.on("GET", "/echo", function(request, response){
  var body = '<html>' +
  '<head><title>Node.js Echo</title></head>' +
  '<body>' +
  '<form method="POST">' +

  '<input type="text" name="msg"/>' +
  '<input type="submit" value="echo"/>' +
  '</form>' +
  '</body></html>';

  response.writeHead(200, {"Content-Type": "text/html"});
  response.write(body);
  response.end();
});
```

We will add an event handler to the same path (/echo), but this time, to handle a GET request. In the handler, we will return an HTML page with a form to post to the same path.

Add these two handlers to our route-handlers.js and execute it with Node.js. To open our form, go to http://localhost:9999/echo; then, to trigger our handler, type in a message in the form's textbox and click on the **echo** button. This will post the content of the form, and in response we will see msg=<your text> in the browser.

Creating our own Modules

Modules are the basic building blocks of Node.js applications. With all our changes, our file is becoming a bit clumsy; moreover, we are putting our infrastructure (server and router) with the application logic (the handlers) in the same place. As mentioned earlier, Node.js builds on the CommonJS module system. In Node.js, a module and a file have a one-to-one relation. Let us move the server and router to their own modules. Save the following in a file called server.js:

```
var http = require("http");
var url = require("url");

function onRequest(request, response) {
  var pathname = url.parse(request.url).pathname;
```

```
    console.log("Request for " + request.method + pathname +
  " received.");
  if(typeof(routes[request.method + pathname])==='function'){
    routes[request.method + pathname](request, response);
  }
  else{
    response.writeHead(404, {"Content-Type": "text/plain"});
    response.end("404 Not Found");
  }
}

var routes = {};

exports.forRoute = function(method, path, handler){
  routes[method + path] = handler;
};

exports.start = function(){
  http.createServer(onRequest).listen(9999);
  console.log("Server has started.");
};
```

Most of the logical aspects of the code remain the same, but we have made some very subtle structural changes. The first one is that we have taken the routes out of the `route` object. Any variables declared in the file are available within the module and are not accessible from outside the module.

```
if(typeof(routes[request.method + pathname])==='function'){
  routes[request.method + pathname](request, response);
}
```

As the `route` object is gone, we can now directly access the routes within the module and not through the `route` object.

The other and more obvious change is `exports`. Since nothing from within the module is available outside the module, we have to add the methods/objects that we want to expose to the implicit `exports` object. Ideally, you should expose only those methods relevant to the end user of your module.

```
exports.forRoute = function(method, path, handler){
  routes[method + path] = handler;
};

exports.start = function(){
  http.createServer(onRequest).listen(9999);
  console.log("Server has started.");
}
```

We are exposing two methods from our module: the `forRoute` method (originally, the `on` method in the `route` object), and the `start` method that wraps the code to start the HTTP server. We also move the application logic to its own module called `app.js`, which is shown in the following code snippet:

```
var server = require("./server.js");
server.forRoute("GET", "/start", function(request, response){
  response.writeHead(200, {"Content-Type": "text/plain"});
  response.write("Hello");
  response.end();
});

server.forRoute("GET", "/finish", function(request, response){
  response.writeHead(200, {"Content-Type": "text/plain"});
  response.write("Goodbye");
  response.end();
});

server.forRoute("POST", "/echo", function(request, response){

  var incoming = "";

  request.on('data', function(chunk) {
    incoming += chunk.toString();
  });

  request.on('end', function(){
    response.writeHead(200, {"Content-Type": "text/plain"});
    response.write(incoming);
    response.end();
  });
});

server.forRoute("GET", "/echo", function(request, response){
  var body = '<html>' +
  '<head><title>Node.js Echo</title></head>' +
  '<body>' +
  '<form method="POST">' +
  '<input type="text" name="msg"/>' +
  '<input type="submit" value="echo"/>' +
  '</form>' +
  '</body></html>';
```

```
      response.writeHead(200, {"Content-Type": "text/html"});
      response.write(body);
      response.end();
    });

    server.start();
```

Again, the logical aspects remain unchanged; the changes are only in the structure.

```
    var server = require("./server.js");
```

The previous line, which is also the first line in the previous code snippet, shows us how our server module is loaded. This is similar to loading core modules like HTTP or URL, but here we are loading the module and passing its filename. The object created by this `require` method, the `server` object, will have two methods that will be exposed: `forRoute` and `start`.

Next, we replace all the calls to `route.on` with the `server.forRoute` method. . And finally, we call the `server.start` method to start the HTTP server.

```
    server.start();
```

Serving files

We can see that it's not very intuitive or easy to write HTML pages with our current infrastructure. Writing the HTML in the JS code as strings is not fun. We would like to serve the HTML content from the HTML files. We will begin with taking in two modules, which we will need to read from a file (on the disk) in our `app` module:

```
    var path = require('path');
    var fs = require('fs');
```

The first one, `path`, is the module we use to work with paths, and `fs` is the module used to interact with the filesystem. The next step is to get the path to the application's root.

```
    var root = __dirname;
```

`__dirname` is a variable managed by Node.js and has the absolute path to the directory of the Node.js application script. Now, we add the method that will be doing the heavy work of reading the file and sending it to the browser. Add this method to `app.js`:

```
    var serveStatic = function(response, file){
      var fileToServe = path.join(root, file);
      var stream = fs.createReadStream(fileToServe);
```

```
    stream.on('data', function(chunk){
      response.write(chunk);
    });

    stream.on('end', function(){
      response.end();
    });
}
```

The `serveStatic` method that we have created accepts two arguments, the HTTP response object and the file path to serve.

```
    var fileToServe = path.join(root, file);
```

We append the file path to our root path to build the absolute path of the file to serve. Here we are implicitly assuming that all the files to be served are relative to the Node.js application root; this will prevent a file outside the application from being served by mistake. Node.js handles I/O as streams. We can see that this is similar to the way it handles the incoming POST data.

```
    var stream = fs.createReadStream(fileToServe);
```

We use `createReadStream` from the `fs` module to create a stream that reads from the file. This stream again demonstrates the non-blocking, asynchronous, and event-driven approach of Node.js.

```
    stream.on('data', function(chunk){
      response.write(chunk);
    });
```

The stream works as an event emitter, triggering the `'data'` event when there is new data on the stream. This allows the application to continue with the other processing activities, without having to wait for the data to be read. What we are doing here is, we are writing the data we receive on every read to the response stream.

```
    stream.on('end', function(){
      response.end();
    });
```

Once all the data from the file is read and the stream gets an EOF, it will trigger the `'end'` event. We will call end on our response as well. Finally, we will modify the GET handler `"/echo"` to serve from a file called `echo.html`, and write the content of the HTML to be served to that file.

```
    server.forRoute("GET", "/echo", function(request, response){
      serveStatic(response, "echo.html");
    });
```

We have removed all the code to build the `response` string, replacing it with a call to `serveStatic` to serve `echo.html`.

```html
<html>
  <head>
    <title>Node.js Echo</title>
  </head>
  <body>
    <form method="POST">
      <input type="text" name="msg"/>
      <input type="submit" value="echo"/>
    </form>
  </body>
</html>
```

The content that we were previously building as a string is now written to this file. Once we make these changes and run `app.js` with Node.js, you should be able to see the form on `http://localhost:9999/echo` retaining its original functionality.

Those familiar with Unix-like operating systems will realize that the functionality we just implemented to read from one stream and write to another can also implemented by using pipes (`|`). It shouldn't come as a surprise that Node.js provides a high-level function to do exactly the same.

Using the `pipe` method provided on `stream` in Node, we can modify the `serveStatic` method as follows:

```js
var serveStatic = function(response, file){
  var fileToServe = path.join(root, file);
  var stream = fs.createReadStream(fileToServe);
  stream.pipe(response);
}
```

Here we are replacing the data and end event handlers using `stream.pipe(response)`.

Third party modules and Express JS

Now that we have built a router of our own and understand the basics of Node.js, it is time to get introduced to one of the most widely-used frameworks for Node.js, Express (`http://expressjs.com`). Node.js provides the infrastructural components to build a web application, but there is too much stuff to handle. Therein lies the role of the web frameworks. There are quite a few web frameworks that provide a higher level of abstraction for building applications on Node. You can see a list of most of them here:

`https://github.com/joyent/node/wiki/Modules#wiki-web-frameworks-full`

Express is a web application framework for Node, built over the Connect middleware, that provides many more helpers and structural aspects to build our web applications.

To get started with the Express framework, we need to install it using npm, the Node.js package manager.

```
sudo npm install -g express
```

The previous command will install Express as a global (-g) module and make express available as a command. Let us create an Express app:

```
express hello-express
```

This will create a folder called hello-express with certain files and folders in it. Let us see and understand these files.

The first file to understand is package.json. This is the file that defines a Node.js application package. It has the application metadata such as the name, description, and version. More importantly, it has the module dependencies listed. The dependency list is used by npm to download the required modules.

```
{
  "name": "application-name",
  "version": "0.0.1",
  "private": true,
  "scripts": {
    "start": "node app"
  },
  "dependencies": {
    "express": "3.1.0",
    "jade": "*"
  }
}
```

The most important things in your package.json are the name and version fields. These fields are required, and together, they form a unique identifier for a particular release of the package. To begin with, let us change the name of our package to hello-express. The version field consists of the following (in the same order):

- A number (major version)
- A period
- A number (minor version)
- A period
- A number (patch version)
- Optional: a hyphen, followed by a number (build)
- Optional: a collection of pretty much any non-whitespace characters (tag)

If we set `private` to true, npm will not publish it to a repository. This ensures that you don't end up publishing your code to a public repository by mistake.

The `scripts` object has a mapping of commands to those points in the application lifecycle at which they should be run. In this package, we are telling Node.js that it should run the `node app` command when the application is started with npm. There are some predefined lifecycle commands, such as `start`, `stop`, `restart`, and `test`, which can be run using `npm <command>` like `npm start`.

You can also run arbitrary commands using `run-script`. For this, you add the command to the `scripts` object and then run it as `npm run-script <command>`.

And finally — the most interesting part of the package that brings in the magic — `dependencies`. This object is a mapping of the name and version of your dependency packages and will be used by npm to pull in all the required dependencies.

In our package, `express` has already defined the dependency on Express and Jade. To pull in these dependencies, run the following command:

```
npm install
```

The output will list all the dependencies it downloaded.

jade@0.27.2 node_modules/jade

├── **commander@0.6.1**

└── **mkdirp@0.3.0**

express@3.0.0rc2 node_modules/express

├── **methods@0.0.1**

├── **fresh@0.1.0**

├── **range-parser@0.0.4**

├── **cookie@0.0.4**

├── **crc@0.2.0**

├── **commander@0.6.1**

├── **debug@0.7.0**

├── **mkdirp@0.3.3**

├── **send@0.0.3 (mime@1.2.6)**

└── **connect@2.4.2 (pause@0.0.1, bytes@0.1.0, qs@0.4.2, formidable@1.0.11)**

The dependencies will be placed in a folder called node_modules.

Next, we will take a look at the application file app.js:

```
var express = require('express')
  , routes = require('./routes')
  , http = require('http')
  , path = require('path');

var app = express();

app.configure(function(){
  app.set('port', process.env.PORT || 3000);
  app.set('views', __dirname + '/views');
  app.set('view engine', 'jade');
  app.use(express.favicon());
  app.use(express.logger('dev'));
  app.use(express.bodyParser());
  app.use(express.methodOverride());
  app.use(app.router);
  app.use(express.static(path.join(__dirname, 'public')));
});

app.configure('development', function(){
  app.use(express.errorHandler());
});

app.get('/', routes.index);

http.createServer(app).listen(app.get('port'), function(){
  console.log("Express server listening on port " +
app.get('port'));
});
```

In the first few lines, Node.js loads the modules required for us to work with. We are already familiar with `http` and `path`. The `express` module brings in the Express framework. And one more module that we are loading in is `./routes`, which will load the module defined in the local `routes` folder, defined by `./routes/index.js`. The following code snippet focuses on the first few lines of the previous code snippet:

```
var express = require('express')
  , routes = require('./routes')
  , http = require('http')
  , path = require('path');
```

In the next line, it instantiates the Express framework as an app:

```
var app = express();
```

Then comes the application configuration:

```
app.configure(function(){

});
```

In the previous few lines, we are defining a function that will configure the app. The signature for `app.configure` is `app.configure([env], callback)`, where `env` is the runtime environment variable *or* the production environment variable, as is defined by `process.env.NODE_ENV`. When we don't specify `env`, it will be set for all environments.

The following settings have been provided to alter how Express behaves:

- `env`: Environment mode, defaults to `process.env.NODE_ENV` or "development"
- `trust proxy`: Enables reverse proxy support, disabled by default
- `jsonp callback`: Enables JSONP callback support, enabled by default
- `jsonp callback name`: Changes the default callback name of `?callback=`
- `json replacer`: JSON replacer callback, `null` by default
- `json spaces`: JSON response spaces for formatting; defaults to `2` in development, `0` in production
- `case sensitive routing`: Enables case sensitivity, disabled by default, treating `/Foo` and `/foo` as the same
- `strict routing`: Enables strict routing, by default `/foo` and `/foo/` are treated the same by the router

- `view cache`: Enables view template compilation caching, enabled in production by default
- `view engine`: The default engine extension to use when omitted
- `views`: The view directory path

The following code snippet demonstrates how to assign settings to an application:

```
app.set('port', process.env.PORT || 3000);
app.set('views', __dirname + '/views');
app.set('view engine', 'jade');
```

The settings used by the application here are `port`, `views`, and `view engine`, specifying that the application should run on port `3000`, the views will be placed in the `views` folder, and the engine to be used is Jade. We will see more about views later. Certain features can also be specified, as shown in the following snippet:

```
app.use(express.favicon());
app.use(express.logger('dev'));
app.use(express.bodyParser());
app.use(express.methodOverride());
app.use(app.router);
app.use(express.static(path.join(__dirname, 'public')));
```

As Express builds over Connect middleware, it brings in a lot of existing functionality from Connect. Connect's `use` method configures the app to utilize the given middleware handle for the given route, where the route defaults to /. You can see the list of middleware provided by Connect at `http://www.senchalabs.org/connect/`.

Let us walk through the middleware components being used here. The Favicon middleware will serve the favicon for the application. The Logger middleware logs requests in a custom format.

The Body parser parses the request bodies supporting different formats; this includes `application/json`, `application/x-www-form-urlencoded`, and `multipart/form-data`.

Method Override enables the faux HTTP method support. This means that if we would like to stimulate the `DELETE` and `PUT` method calls to our application, we can do it by adding a `_method` parameter to the request.

`app.router` provides an enhanced version of Connect's `router` module. Basically, this is the component that determines what to do when we use routing methods like `app.get`. The last middleware, Static, provides a static file server and configures it, serving files from the `public` directory.

For the development environment, the following two lines of code show how to set up the Error handler middleware so as to provide stack traces and error messages in the responses.

```
app.configure('development', function(){
  app.use(express.errorHandler());
});
```

The next line configures the router to route / to be handled by the index method in the routes module:

```
app.get('/', routes.index);
```

At the end, we start the HTTP server configured to use the app instance that we just configured.

```
http.createServer(app).listen(app.get('port'), function(){
  console.log("Express server listening on port " + app.get('port'));
});
```

In the configuration of the app, we saw some folders coming into play, namely, routes, views, and public.

routes is a module that we will be writing all our handlers to. In the case of /, we have mapped it to serve from the index method, using the routes.index method. If you open routes/index.js, you will see that index is a method exposed from this module.

```
exports.index = function(req, res){
  res.render('index', { title: 'Express' });
};
```

This function signature is similar to the handlers we wrote. It is a function that takes a request and response as parameters. Here we are using the Express method response.render, which will render the mentioned view using the second parameter as the model or data.

The views are present in the views folder and use the Jade (http://jade-lang.com/) view engine. Jade is a high-performance template engine, heavily influenced by Haml (http://haml.info/), and implemented with JavaScript for Node.js. Like many modern HTML generation engines, Jade tries to make the UI code easier, cleaner, and simpler, getting rid of the inline code and the HTML tags noise.

We will now see the views defined in our Express app. There are two files to see here: layout.jade and index.jade.

`layout.jade`, as the name suggests, is the template for the layout that will be used by the different pages in our application. It may be used to place the common code of the skeleton for the pages in our application, which is shown in the following snippet:

```
doctype 5
html
  head
    title= title
    link(rel='stylesheet', href='/stylesheets/style.css')
  body
    block content
```

In Jade, we don't need the `start` and `end` tags because it identifies the start and end of the tags by the indented blocks. So when we render this Jade file, it will generate the following HTML code:

```
<!DOCTYPE html>
<html>
  <head>
    <title>{TITLE}</title>
    <link rel="stylesheet" href="/stylesheets/style.css" />
  </head>
  <body>{CONTENT}</body>
</html>
```

In the previous piece of code, two things are left undefined, {TITLE} and {CONTENT}. In the Jade template, we define the title as follows:

```
title= title
```

We tell Jade to use the title from the data passed to `render` as `title`. The second thing, {CONTENT}, is defined as block in Jade.

```
block content
```

`block content` is a plugin point provided in the layout template, which can be described by any template extending from it.

`index.jade` inherits from `layout.jade`. In our index handler, we render the index view using the data {title: 'Express'}. Take a look at the following code snippet:

```
extends layout
block content
  h1= title
  p Welcome to #{title}
```

In the previous file, we define the content block to have a h1 and p tags. So, with the given input and because it extends the layout, the Jade engine will generate the following HTML:

```
<!DOCTYPE html>
<html>
  <head>
    <title>Express</title>
    <link rel="stylesheet" href="/stylesheets/style.css" />
  </head>
  <body>
    <h1>Express</h1>
    <p>Welcome to Express</p>
  </body>
</html>
```

We will see more functionality and syntax in Jade as we work on our chat application in the next chapter.

In the HTML code generated, we can see that /stylesheets/style.css is being referred to; this file is served by the static file server we configured in the app. We can find this and the other files in the public folder.

To run this application, we will use npm. Run the following command on the console:

npm start

Then go to http://localhost:3000/.

Summary

In this chapter we were introduced to the Node.js and Express web frameworks. As mentioned earlier, this is in no way a complete introduction to Node.js or Express. To learn more, please refer to the vast documentation available online or any of the books written on Node.js web development.

3
Let's Chat

Beginning with Yahoo! Chat in the early 2000 and up to today's popular Google Talk or Facebook Chat, chatting has been the most popular form of real-time communication on the Internet. In this chapter, we will build a chat room using node and express, which we learned in the previous chapter, and the socket.io library that we will learn in this chapter.

Creating the application

Similar to the way we created our application in the previous chapter, we will create a new `awesome-chat` application by executing the following commands in the command line:

```
$ express awesome-chat
$ cd awesome-chat
$ npm install
```

This will create our application and install the express application dependencies. Open the `package.json` file and change the name to `awesome-chat`, as shown in the following code snippet:

```
{
  "name": "awesome-chat",
  "version": "0.0.1",
  "private": true,
  "scripts": {
    "start": "node app"
  },
  "dependencies": {
    "express": "3.0.0rc2express": "3.x",
    "jade": "*"
  }
}
```

Designing the chat room

Let's modify the view to make it look like a chat room. We will need an area to display the messages, a text input for the user to enter the message, and a button to send the message. We will add some aesthetic elements, such as a header, banner, and footer. When we are done, our chat room user interface should look like the one shown in the following screenshot:

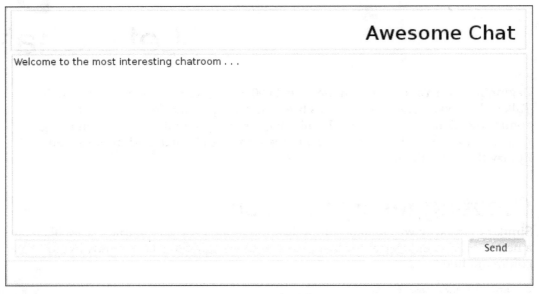

Awesome chat UI

Let's start editing `layout.jade` by adding a header and footer to it:

```
doctype 5
html
  block head
    title= title
    link(rel='stylesheet', href='/stylesheets/style.css')
  body
    header#banner
      h1 Awesome Chat
    block content
    footer Hope you enjoy your stay here
```

The first change we make is to add the `block` keyword before `head`. This makes `head` a block, to which we can append content from the extending pages.

The other change is the addition of a new header and footer. Note that we are using the `header` and `footer` tags from HTML5. This code also introduces us to a new jade syntax. When we write `header#banner`, it will generate headers with `banner` as the `id` value. The generated HTML code will be as follows:

```
<!DOCTYPE html>
<html>
  <head>
    <title>{TITLE}</title>
    <link rel="stylesheet" href="/stylesheets/style.css" />
  </head>
  <body>
    <header id="banner">
      <h1>Awesome Chat</h1>
    </header>
    {CONTENT}
    <footer>
      Hope you enjoy your stay here
    </footer>
  </body>
</html>
```

Next, we will edit `index.jade` to add the message area, message input, and the **Send** button:

```
extends layout
block content
  section#chatroom
    div#messages
    input#message(type='text', placeholder='Enter your message here')
    input#send(type='button', value='Send')
```

Let's run and see what our `awesome-chat` application looks like. Execute the application using `npm` and open `http://localhost:3000/` in the browser:

npm start

Hey, all the elements are there, but it doesn't look right! That's correct; to improve the look and feel of the application, we need to edit the stylesheet, which is located at `public/stylesheets/style.css`.

We can edit it according to our taste. Here is one that works just fine for me:

```
html {
  height: 100%;
}

body {
```

```
    font: 14px "Lucida Grande", Helvetica, Arial, sans-serif;
    margin: 0px;
    padding: 0px;
    height: -moz-calc(100% - 20px);
    height: -webkit-calc(100% - 20px);
    height: calc(100% - 20px);
}

section#chatroom {
    height: -moz-calc(100% - 80px);
    height: -webkit-calc(100% - 80px);
    height: calc(100% - 80px);
    background-color: #EFFFEC;
}

div#messages {
    height: -moz-calc(100% - 35px);
    height: -webkit-calc(100% - 35px);
    height: calc(100% - 35px);
    padding: 10px;
    -moz-box-sizing:border-box;
    -webkit-box-sizing:border-box;
    box-sizing:border-box;
}

input#message {
    width: -moz-calc(100% - 80px);
    width: -webkit-calc(100% - 80px);
    width: calc(100% - 80px);
}

input#send {
    width: 74px;
}

header{
    background-color:#4192C1;
    text-align: right;
    margin-top: 15px;
}

header h1{
    padding: 5px;
    padding-right: 15px;
    color: #FFFFFF;
    margin: 0px;
}
```

```
footer{
    padding: 6px;
    background-color:#4192C1;
    color: #FFFFFF;
    bottom: 0;
    position: absolute;
    width: 100%;
    margin: 0px;
    margin-bottom: 10px;
    -moz-box-sizing:border-box;
    -webkit-box-sizing:border-box;
    box-sizing:border-box;
}

a {
    color: #00B7FF;
}
```

After saving this CSS and refreshing the page, here is what the chat room looks like:

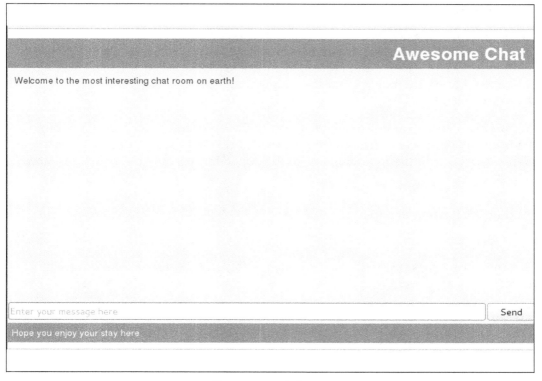

The awesome chat room

Bringing in jQuery

jQuery is almost ubiquitous when it comes to JavaScript libraries, and we will use it in our application too. To add jQuery to our application, let's download the latest release from `http://www.jquery.com/` and save it to `public/javascript/jquery.min.js`. Then, we add the script in `layout.jade` to pull in jQuery to our application's pages:

```
script(type='text/javascript', src='/javascripts/jquery.min.js')
```

Socket.IO

Ever since the onset of web applications, developers have worked towards different ways of getting duplex communication between the server and the browser. Be it using Java, Flash, Comet, or many other workarounds, all aim to do the same. But for the first time, there is a specification to build a full-duplex communication system by using HTML5 WebSockets. **WebSocket** is a revolutionary, new communication feature in the HTML5 specification that defines a full-duplex communication channel operating over the Web through a single socket.

Although the WebSockets RFC is published, it is not, and will never be, available on older browsers that are still in use. Socket.io is an abstraction layer for WebSockets, with Flash, XHR, JSONP, and HTMLFile fallbacks. Socket.io provides an easy server and client library for making real-time, streaming updates between a web server and a browser client.

Socket.io is a node module available through the npm, and we will add it to our package dependencies. The current release of socket.io is `0.9.10`. To add this to our dependencies, add the following line to the dependencies object in `package.json`:

```
"socket.io": "0.9.10"
```

And install it using the npm:

```
$ npm install
```

This will bring socket.io in the `node_modules` folder. Now let's see how we will use it.

Handling events

Since the socket.io framework has components for both the server and the client, we will use these components to code our communication on both the sides. Events emitted on a socket on one side will be handled by the corresponding event handler on the other side. Socket.io is built so that both the sides can send messages or attach handlers to process the incoming messages.

Let's begin by understanding how the messages will flow. It is important to remember that "messages" here are not the actual messages sent and received by users of the chat system, but the messages used for communication by the client and the server. There will be two types of messages, as follows:

- **The system messages**: These messages will be sent by our chat system to the client, like when the user is connected, when others connect, or when users disconnect. Let's identify it with `serverMessage`.

- **The user messages**: These messages will be sent by the client to the server and will actually carry the user's message content in the payload. We will probably want to differentiate between the messages we send and the messages other users send. So let's call them `myMessage` and `userMessage` respectively.

When a user connects for the first time, the server will send a welcome message to the user as a `serverMessage` message.

When a user types in a message and presses the **Send** button, we will send a `userMessage` message from the browser to the server.

On receiving the user message, the server will broadcast this message to all the other users. It will also send back the same message as `myMessage` to the user who originally sent the message.

On receiving any message from the server, the browser will display the contents of the message in the message area.

The server

Now we will implement the server, which will perform the task of relaying the messages, as already mentioned. Create a file in the `routes` folder called `sockets.js` and insert the following code into it:

```
var io = require('socket.io');

exports.initialize = function(server) {
  io = io.listen(server);
  io.sockets.on("connection", function(socket){
    socket.send(JSON.stringify(
      {type:'serverMessage',
        message: 'Welcome to the most interesting chat room on
earth!'}));
    socket.on('message', function(message){
      message= JSON.parse(message);
      if(message.type == "userMessage"){
        socket.broadcast.send(JSON.stringify(message));
        message.type = "myMessage";
        socket.send(JSON.stringify(message));
      }
    });
  });
};
```

In the first line of code (you must be familiar with this by now), we import the `socket.io` module; we will identify this module by the `io` variable.

Since socket.io works with the communication layer, we need to set it up to listen to the HTTP server. The HTTP server can only be accessed from the main application module, so we have to pass `server` to our module before our module can do anything. Hence, we export a method called `initialize` from our module, which will set up the socket.io server and also bind all the message handlers:

```
exports.initialize = function(server) {
  //work to do
}
```

The `initialize` method will accept the HTTP `server` object as a parameter. This is required by socket.io:

```
io = io.listen(server);
```

On the first line of the method, we will pass the server to the socket.io module's `listen` method. The server is an instance of the node HTTP server module; socket. io will configure various handlers on this server. This is the only boilerplate code required to set up socket.io. Next, we need to set up our message handler for socket. io messages.

The first event that our server will receive is a new connection from a new client. This is identified by the `connection` event on the `io.sockets` object and notifies our application that a new client has opened a new connection and all the protocol negotiation (transparent to us) has been completed and now we have a socket to communicate with this client:

```
io.sockets.on("connection", function(socket){
//Add other event handlers to the socket
});
```

The `connection` event handler will be triggered, passing along the socket that was just established. The socket is an event emitter that can trigger different events based on the messages it gets, and we will use this socket also to communicate with the client for which it was created. There are several events exposed, such as the `connection` event to handle events on the server. Let's take a quick look at these events:

- `io.sockets.on('connection', function(socket) {})`: Initial connection from a client. The `socket` argument should be used in further communication with the client.

- `socket.on('message', function(message, callback) {})`: The `message` handler is triggered when a message sent with `socket.send` is received. The `message` parameter is the message sent, and `callback` is an optional acknowledgment function.

- `socket.on('anything', function(data) {})`: The `anything` event can be any event except the reserved events.

- `socket.on('disconnect', function() {})`: This event is fired when the socket disconnects.

Now that we have seen how to handle the socket events, let's see how we can send messages from the server to the client:

```
socket.send(JSON.stringify(
  {type:'serverMessage',
    message: 'Welcome to the most interesting chat room on
earth!'}));
```

The `socket.send` method will send the message on the socket, which will be triggering the `message` event on the client. The message sent has to be a string, so we will use `JSON.stringify` to send the data for the message as a string. Here our message has two parts, a type and a message.

One part of our task is over, we are now able to welcome the user. The next task is to handle the user messages when they come in. For this, we set a `message` event handler on the socket:

```
socket.on('message', function(message){
    message= JSON.parse(message);

    if(message.type == "userMessage"){
      socket.broadcast.send(JSON.stringify(message));
      message.type = "myMessage";
      socket.send(JSON.stringify(message));
    }
});
```

Just like any other event connector, `socket.on` will take two parameters, namely the event to handle and the event handler for it. In this case, unlike the `io.sockets.on` event, this event handler will receive the message as the parameter and not the socket.

Since the message is a string, we will parse the message's JSON string to create a `message` object. If this is a message sent by the user, this message will be of the type `userMessage`, and that is what we check.

Now, we have to send out this message to all the connected users. For this, socket. io provides us with a `broadcast` object. When we send the message using the `broadcast` object, it will be sent to all the clients that are connected, except to the one for which this socket was created. The syntax for sending the message here is the same; the difference is that it is called on the `broadcast` object, referred to as message flags in socket.io, instead of the socket itself.

Also, we want to send back the same content to the client that sent this message, but just change the type to `myMessage`. For this, we send the message directly on the socket.

That's it. We have written the code for the server; but now we have to actually initialize this server. To do this, modify the server creation in `app.js` to set the `server` variable, as shown in the following code snippet:

```
var server = http.createServer(app).listen(app.get('port'),
  function(){
    console.log("Express server listening on port " + app.
get('port'));
  });
```

Now that we have modified the HTTP server, we can call the socket module's `initialize` method, passing this server as a parameter to it. Add the following line to the end of `app.js`:

```
require('./routes/sockets.js').initialize(server);
```

The client

Now that we have seen how the server works, let's see what the client does. The best part of socket.io is that it provides us the same API on the server and the client. For our chat logic on the client, let's create a file called `chat.js` in the `public/javascripts` folder and add the following code to it:

```
var socket = io.connect('/');

socket.on('message', function (data) {
  data = JSON.parse(data);
  $('#messages').append('<div class="'+data.type+'">' + data.message +
'</div>');
});

$(function(){
  $('#send').click(function(){
    var data = {
      message: $('#message').val(),
      type:'userMessage'
    };
    socket.send(JSON.stringify(data));
    $('#message').val('');
  });
});
```

The first step in starting the chat is to connect to the server:

```
var socket = io.connect('/');
```

This will send a connection request to the server from which the page was loaded. This will also negotiate the actual transport protocol and will finally result in the `connection` event being triggered on the server app.

The following code snippet connects the event handler for the `message` event:

```
socket.on('message', function (data) {
  data = JSON.parse(data);
  $('#messages').append('<div class="'+data.type+'">' + data.message +
'</div>');
});
```

All we have to do with the incoming message is to append it to the messages area. We are adding one additional detail here by setting the class property for the newly appended div tag to be of the same type as that of the message. We can later use this to give a different look to the different types of messages.

The last thing to do on the client side is to send the messages from the user. This will be done when the user writes his/her message in the message box and clicks the **Send** button. So, let's add an event handler to the **Send** button. The important thing about UI elements' event handlers is that they should be attached once the element is added to the document, that is, after it is created and ready. jQuery provides a convenient method to detect when the document is ready and adds a handler function to execute. There are two ways to do this; one is the following:

```
$(document).ready(function(){
   //Execute once the document is ready
});
```

The shortcut for the same is as follows:

```
$(function(){
   //Execute once the document is ready
});
```

Once the document is ready, we attach the event handler to the click event of the **Send** button:

```
$(function(){
  $('#send').click(function(){
    var data = {
      message: $('#message').val(),
      type:'userMessage'
    };
    socket.send(JSON.stringify(data));
    $('#message').val('');
  });
});
```

On clicking the **Send** button, we create our data object, setting the content of the message box as message, and type as userMessage. We can then use the socket. send method to send this data to the server. As you can see from the preceding code snippet, the syntax for sending messages from the client is the same as that of the server, and here too the message will be sent as a sting, which we create using JSON.stringify(data).

Like the `connection` event and other predefined events on the server, we have some predefined events on the client too. These are as follows:

- `socket.on('connect', function () {})`: The `connect` event is emitted when the socket is connected successfully.

- `socket.on('connecting', function () {})`:The `connecting` event is emitted when the socket is attempting to connect with the server.

- `socket.on('disconnect', function () {})`: The `disconnect` event is emitted when the socket is disconnected.

- `socket.on('connect_failed', function () {})`: The `connect_failed` event is emitted when socket.io fails to establish a connection to the server and has no more transports to fall back to.

- `socket.on('error', function () {})`: The `error` event is emitted when an error occurs and it cannot be handled by the other event types.

- `socket.on('message', function (message, callback) {})`: The `message` event is emitted when a message sent by using `socket.send` is received. The `message` parameter is the sent message, and `callback` is an optional acknowledgment function.

- `socket.on('anything', function(data, callback) {})`: The `anything` event can be any event except the reserved events. The `data` parameter represents the data, and `callback` can be used to send a reply.

- `socket.on('reconnect_failed', function () {})`: The `reconnect_failed` event is emitted when socket.io fails to reestablish a working connection after the connection was dropped.

- `socket.on('reconnect', function () {})`: The `reconnect` event is emitted when socket.io is successfully reconnected to the server.

- `socket.on('reconnecting', function () {})`: The `reconnecting` event is emitted when the socket is attempting to reconnect with the server.

The last task to be done on the client side is to add socket.io and the chat scripts to our chat room page. Since these will not be used on every page, instead of adding them to `layout.jade`, we will add these to `index.jade`.

Remember the change we had made to `layout.jade`, changing the code from `head` to `block head`? It will allow us to append the content from `index.jade` to the `head` tag:

```
block append head
    script(type='text/javascript', src='/socket.io/socket.io.js')
    script(type='text/javascript', src='/javascripts/chat.js')
```

In the following line of code, we are using Jade's functionality to append content to a block in an inherited template from the child element. This is done using the `append` keyword. The syntax is as follows:

```
block append <blockname>
```

The shorter form is as follows:

```
append <blockname>
```

The next two lines of code add the script tags by adding `socket.io.js` and `chat.js` to our page. You might be wondering where the `/socket.io/socket.io.js` file comes from, since we neither add it and nor does it exist on the filesystem. This is part of the magic done by `io.listen` on the server. It creates a handler on the server to serve the `socket.io.js` script file.

And we are ready. Restart the node server and browse to `http://localhost:3000/` to open the chat room. You will see the welcome message, **Welcome to the most interesting chat room on earth!**, being displayed in the message area.

To see how our chat application works, open it in two separate browser instances. Now you can enter your message in the message box in one of the browsers and click **Send**. You will see it appear on the message area of both the browsers.

Congratulations! We now have a chat room. If you deploy it to a server or allow access to port `3000` on your system, you can invite your friends to chat.

Summary

In this chapter, we learned about socket.io and worked through some very basic concepts and APIs provided by socket.io. We also saw how to set up socket.io on the server and the client, and how to send and receive messages. While doing so, we also built a chat room application using all that we have learned up to this point.

In the next chapter we will build upon the application that we have created to add other features such as session data, multiple chat rooms, namespacing, and authentication while getting acquainted with the related features of socket.io.

4
Making It More Fun!

In the previous chapter, we created a chat room. In this chapter, we are going to improve on that chat room by giving our users a name, having multiple chat rooms, and integrating the express and socket.io sessions.

Giving names to users

Without a name for our users, chatting becomes difficult. It is impossible to identify who sent the message. So let us provide our users with a method by which they can set a nickname for themselves, so that a message from them can be identified with their name.

We have already worked with the message event in socket.io to send and receive messages. We also saw the socket.io module's predefined events. In this section, we will learn more about those events and also see how we can work with our own events. We will also see how we can save some information for the session.

Let us start by creating the user interface required for accepting a name from the user when they come to our chat room. To do this, we will modify the index.jade file by adding the following code to it:

```
//EXISTING LAYOUT
  section#nameform.modal
    div.backdrop
    div.popup
      div.pophead Please enter a nickname
      div.popbody
        input#nickname(type='text')
        input#setname(type='button', value='Set Name')
```

What we are doing here is adding a new section for the modal overlay. This section has a backdrop div tag and then a div tag for the actual form. The look and feel of this will again be defined in the style.css file, so let's update that too. Refer to the following code block while modifying the stylesheet:

```
//EXISTING CSS
.modal{
  -moz-box-sizing: border-box;
  -webkit-box-sizing: border-box;
  box-sizing: border-box;
  -moz-box-sizing: border-box;
  height: -moz-calc(100% - 102px);
  height: -webkit-calc(100% - 102px);
  height: calc(100% - 102px);
  left: 0;
  position: absolute;
  top: 62px;
  width: 100%;
  z-index: 1000;
}

.backdrop{
  width: 100%;
  height:100%;
  background-color: #777777;
}

.popup {
  position: absolute;
  height: 100px;
  width: 300px;
  left: -moz-calc(50% - 150px);
  left: -webkit-calc(50% - 150px);
  left: calc(50% - 150px);
  top: -moz-calc(50% - 50px);
  top: -webkit-calc(50% - 50px);
  top: calc(50% - 50px);
  background: #FFFFFF;
}

.pophead {
  background-color: #4192C1;
  color: #FFFFFF;
  font-weight: bold;
  padding: 8px 3px;
  vertical-align: middle;
}

.popbody {
  padding: 10px 5px;
}
```

Now when we refresh the UI, it will look like this:

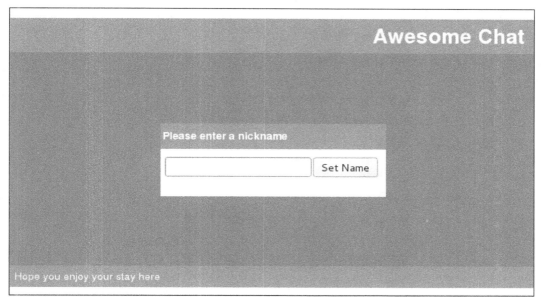

The username form

Next, what we will want to do is when the user enters a name and clicks on the **Set Name** button, send the name to the server, store it there, and prefix it to every message sent by that user. First, we will change the document ready handler to attach an event handler to the **Set Name** button. For this, edit `public/javascripts/chat.js`:

```
$(function(){
  $('#setname').click(function(){
    socket.emit("set_name", {name: $('#nickname').val()});
  });
});
```

In the previous code, we see a new socket.io API and concept, namely `socket.emit`. This is used to trigger custom events. The call for `emit` is as follows:

```
socket.emit(<event_name>, <event_data>);
```

We trigger a `set_name` event and pass on the value entered in the username box by the user. We also remove the send message event handler from the `socket.emit` declaration. We will come back to this later.

The events emitted on a socket on one side (server) will be handled on the other side of the socket (client). In our case, that is, in the previous code snippet, we trigger the set_name event on the client, so we will handle it on the server. To do this, we will edit routes/sockets.js as follows:

```
var io = require('socket.io');

exports.initialize = function(server) {
  io = io.listen(server);
  io.sockets.on("connection", function(socket){
    socket.on('message', function(message){
      message= JSON.parse(message);
      if(message.type == "userMessage"){
        socket.get('nickname', function(err, nickname){
          message.username=nickname;
          socket.broadcast.send(JSON.stringify(message));
          message.type = "myMessage";
          socket.send(JSON.stringify(message));
        });
      }
    });
    socket.on("set_name", function(data){
      socket.set('nickname', data.name, function(){
        socket.emit('name_set', data);
      socket.send(JSON.stringify({type:'serverMessage',
      message: 'Welcome to the most interesting chat room on earth!'}));
      });
    });
  });
}
```

In the practice of keeping it simple, socket.io uses the same `socket.on` API, which we used earlier to handle the `connection` or `message` events, to handle custom events. The data passed to the handler function will contain the data we had sent when we triggered the event.

This brings us to a new feature of socket.io, that is, attaching additional information to the socket for the session. This is achieved using the `socket.set` function. The call for this function is as follows:

```
socket.set(<name>, <value>, <optional_callback>);
```

In the preceding line of code, `<name>` is the name of the key we want to set and `<value>` is the value we want to set. The call to `set` is asynchronous; it won't be blocked till the value has been set. To perform an action where you want to ensure that the value has been set, we can pass a callback to the `set` method. In the previous code, we are passing the `callback` function that will emit another `name_set` custom event, and will also send the welcome message. Like the `set_name` event, the `name_set` event will be handled on the other side of the socket, which in this case is the client.

This is great. Now that the name is set, let us put it to some real use by showing it with every message so that people in our chat room know who sent the message.

To get a value set on the socket, socket.io provides a `get` method. We will use this `get` method to get the username from the socket and append it to the previous message.

Let us rework `public/javscripts/chat.js` to handle the `name_set` event and then start the actual communication:

```javascript
var socket = io.connect('/');

socket.on('name_set', function(data){
  $('#nameform').hide();
  $('#messages').append('<div class="systemMessage">' +
                                         'Hello '+data.name+'</div>');
  $('#send').click(function(){
    var data = {
      message: $('#message').val(),
      type:'userMessage'
    };
    socket.send(JSON.stringify(data));
    $('#message').val('');
  });
```

```
socket.on('message', function (data) {
  data = JSON.parse(data);
  if(data.username){
    $('#messages').append('<div class="'+data.type+
                  '"><span class="name">' +
               data.username + ":</span> " +
               data.message + '</div>');
  }else{
    $('#messages').append('<div class="'+data.type+'">' +
                               data.message +
'</div>');
  }
});
});


$(function(){

  $('#setname').click(function(){

    socket.emit("set_name", {name: $('#nickname').val()});

  });

});
```

In the previous code snippet, we add two new lines of code to hide the overlay and to append the greeting to the messages area. Apart from this, we have also moved the code to handle the sending and receiving of messages to this handler, so that it is set up only after the user has set the name and avoids people from just hiding the overlay using Firebug or other similar tools. There is one last change in the message received handler; we need to check for the presence of a username in the incoming data and prefix it to the displayed message if it is.

To see the code in action, let's restart our node server and refresh the browser. Once you enter the name, it will bring up the chat room and show the greeting with the name you just entered along with the welcome message:

Greeting with name

Open our chat room in another browser window and sign in as **Friend** this time. Enter a message in the new message box and click **Send**. The message appears in the message area in both the browsers. Try it from the first chat room you have opened:

Chat with names

More on events

In the previous section, we saw how we can use custom events over a socket. The interesting thing is that just like your messages, events can also be broadcast. Let us see how we can use an event broadcast to announce the entry of a participant in our chat room.

For this, the first thing we will do is start emitting a new `user_entered` event from the server, with the name of the user in the data once the user has joined the chat. Let us change our `routes/socket.js` file to do this. We will add our code to broadcast the `user_entered` event once the username is set.

```
socket.on("set_name", function(data){
  socket.set('nickname', data.name, function(){
     socket.emit('name_set', data);
  socket.send(JSON.stringify({type:'serverMessage',
            message: 'Welcome to the most interesting" +
                                         "chat room on
earth!'}));
    socket.broadcast.emit('user_entered', data);
   });
 });
```

To send a broadcast to all the clients connected on this socket, we use the `emit` method, but on `socket.broadcast` rather than on `socket` itself. The signature of the method is the same.

Now, the `user_entered` event will be sent to all the connected clients, so we will need to add an event handler in the client `chat.js` file.

```
socket.on('name_set', function(data){

  // EXISTING CODE

  socket.on("user_entered", function(user){
    $('#messages').append('<div class="systemMessage">' +
                        user.name + ' has joined the room.' + '</
div>');
  });
});
```

Here, we are adding an event handler for the user_entered event and then displaying the message to the user. Let us start our server once again and log in to our chat room:

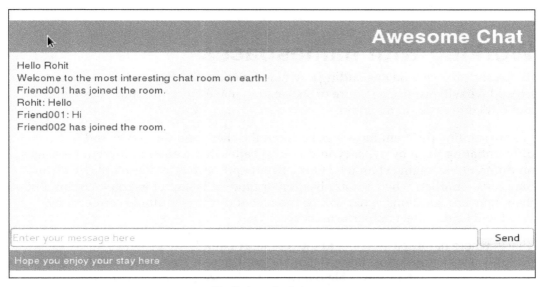

The first user's chat room

Now open another browser window and log in with a different name:

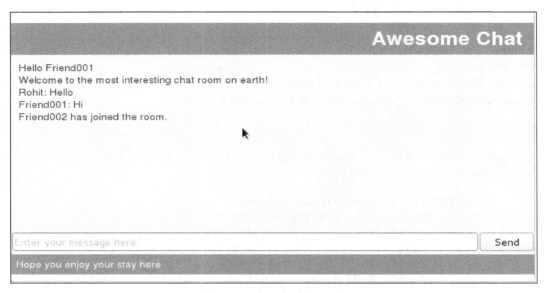

The second user's chat room

As you will notice, in the first user's window, we will see the entrance message for both **Friend001** and **Friend002**, and for **Friend002** in the second user's (**Friend001**) window.

Working with namespaces

In this section, we won't be adding any new functionality to our chat room, but instead we will just use a feature of socket.io to make our application design better and our code easier to maintain.

We are sending different messages between the client and the server and differentiating them by `type`. Wouldn't it be better that we send different messages on different messaging channels? Our current approach also doesn't play well and may cause conflicts when our application or module is part of a larger system. But then there are questions, what will be the cost of opening multiple connections? What will be the effect on performance?

This is where namespaces come to the rescue. A namespace provides a way to multiply a socket.io connection, so that we get different channels for different types of messages without adding a big overhead to the system and its performance. Let us see how we can use namespaces in our chat system.

In our chat application, we have two different types of messages or events being sent. These are infrastructural, such as setting the name and welcome messages, and communication between the users.

So let us go ahead and create two namespaces, namely `chat_com` and `chat_infra`. We will send the communication messages (user messages) on `chat_com` and the infrastructural messages (welcome, user entry, and so on) on `chat_infra`. For this, let us first edit the `socket.js` file, which is on the server:

```
var io = require('socket.io');

exports.initialize = function (server) {
  io = io.listen(server);

  var chatInfra = io.of("/chat_infra")
      .on("connection", function(socket){
        socket.on("set_name", function (data) {
          socket.set('nickname', data.name, function () {
            socket.emit('name_set', data);
            socket.send(JSON.stringify({type:'serverMessage',
              message:'Welcome to the most interesting ' +
              'chat room on earth!'}));
            socket.broadcast.emit('user_entered', data);
```

```
              });
            });
          });

    var chatCom = io.of("/chat_com")
        .on("connection", function (socket) {
          socket.on('message', function (message) {
            message = JSON.parse(message);
            if (message.type == "userMessage") {
              socket.get('nickname', function (err, nickname) {
                message.username = nickname;
                socket.broadcast.send(JSON.stringify(message));
                message.type = "myMessage";
                socket.send(JSON.stringify(message));
              });
            }
          });
        });
    }
```

As we can see from the preceding code, most of the code remains the same, apart from the highlighted snippets and some code reorganization.

What we are doing here is separating the messages and events into two code blocks corresponding to their namespaces. We use the io.of method to create a new namespace. Upon creation of the namespace, it can be used as any socket's object.

In our case, we are creating two namespaces and adding a connection event handler to both of them. One for chat_infra, as shown in the following code snippet:

```
    var chatInfra = io.of("/chat_infra")
        .on("connection", function(socket){
```

And another for chat_com:

```
    var chatCom = io.of("/chat_com")
        .on("connection", function (socket) {
```

Once the connection is established, we will get a socket object in the connection event handler, which we will use just as we did earlier. In case of chat_infra, we add all the messaging and events that are not part of the user-to-user communication:

```
            socket.on("set_name", function (data) {
              socket.set('nickname', data.name, function () {
                socket.emit('name_set', data);
                socket.send(JSON.stringify({type:'serverMessage',
                  message:'Welcome to the most interesting ' +
                  'chat room on earth!'}));
```

```
            socket.broadcast.emit('user_entered', data);
        });
    });
```

So, we are moving the `set_name` handler, the event emitter for `name_set`, messaging for `serverMessage`, and the event broadcaster for `user_entered` to the `chat_infra` namespace.

```
socket.on('message', function (message) {
    message = JSON.parse(message);
    if (message.type == "userMessage") {
        socket.get('nickname', function (err, nickname) {
            message.username = nickname;
            socket.broadcast.send(JSON.stringify(message));
            message.type = "myMessage";
            socket.send(JSON.stringify(message));
        });
    }
});
```

This leaves only the standard `User` messaging components on the `chat_com` namespace.

Let us now see how this affects our client code:

```
var chatInfra = io.connect('/chat_infra'),
    chatCom = io.connect('/chat_com');

chatInfra.on('name_set', function (data) {
  chatInfra.on("user_entered", function (user) {
    $('#messages').append('<div class="systemMessage">' + user.name
        + ' has joined the room.' + '</div>');
  });

  chatInfra.on('message', function (message) {
    var message = JSON.parse(message);
    $('#messages').append('<div class="' + message.type + '">'
        + message.message + '</div>');
  });

  chatCom.on('message', function (message) {
    var message = JSON.parse(message);
      $('#messages').append('<div class="' +
    message.type + '"><span class="name">' +
    message.username + ':</span> ' +
          message.message + '</div>');
  });

  $('#nameform').hide();
  $('#messages').append('<div class="systemMessage">Hello ' +
```

```
      data.name + '</div>');

  $('#send').click(function () {
    var data = {
      message:$('#message').val(),
      type:'userMessage'
    };
    chatCom.send(JSON.stringify(data));
    $('#message').val('');
  });
});

$(function () {
  $('#setname').click(function () {
    chatInfra.emit("set_name", {name:$('#nickname').val()});
  });
});
```

The first and the most important thing we see in the previous code is that we are connecting two sockets:

```
var chatInfra = io.connect('/chat_infra'),
    chatCom = io.connect('/chat_com');
```

In fact, socket.io will establish a single socket connection and multiplex the two namespaces over it. But establishing these two connections will give us the ability to handle the chat_infra and chat_com namespaces' messages or events separately.

In the following code snippet, we are adding the handlers that correspond to the emitters for chat_infra that we added on the server. The name_set handler will be on the chat_infra namespace:

```
chatInfra.on('name_set', function (data) {
```

We will also do the same for the user_entered handler:

```
chatInfra.on("user_entered", function (user) {
  $('#messages').append('<div class="systemMessage">' + user.name
      + ' has joined the room.' + '</div>');
});
```

Next, we add the on handler to listen for the messages on chat_infra; this will receive all the server messages:

```
chatInfra.on('message', function (message) {
  var message = JSON.parse(message);
  $('#messages').append('<div class="' + message.type + '">'
      + message.message + '</div>');
});
```

We also emit the `set_name` event on `chat_infra`:

```
chatInfra.emit("set_name", {name:$('#nickname').val()});
```

On the `chat_com` namespace, we send the user message, as shown in the following code:

```
$('#send').click(function () {
    var data = {
        message:$('#message').val(),
        type:'userMessage'
    };
    chatCom.send(JSON.stringify(data));
```

Also, we will attach the handler to receive the user messages relayed from the server by using the following code snippet:

```
chatCom.on('message', function (message) {
    var message = JSON.parse(message);
    $('#messages').append('<div class="' +
    message.type + '"><span class="name">' +
    message.username + ':</span> ' +
        message.message + '</div>');
});
```

Now that we understand namespaces and have made use of them to clean up our design and code, let us go ahead and add some new features.

Rooms

In this section we will use another multiplexing feature of socket.io, called **rooms**. And we will use it to do just what the name says, create rooms. A chat room will be very noisy and confusing if everyone in the network is chatting in the same room. So as the first step, let's move our chat away from the landing page of our website to `/chatroom`. For this, we should move our code from `index.jade` to `chatroom.jade` and put the following code in `index.jade`:

```
extends layout

block content
  section#welcome
    div Welcome
    a#startchat(type="button", class="btn", href="/chatroom") Start
now
```

Basically, we will create a landing page with a welcome message and a link to go to the chat room. Let's also add the following styles for the landing page in `style.css`:

```css
#welcome div{
  font-family: fantasy;
  font-size: 100px;
  margin-left: 20px;
  margin-top: 100px;
}


.btn {
    background-color: #5BB75B;
    background-image: linear-gradient(to bottom, #62C462, #51A351);
    background-repeat: repeat-x;
    border-color: rgba(0, 0, 0, 0.1) rgba(0, 0, 0, 0.1) rgba(0, 0, 0, 0.25);
    color: #FFFFFF;
    text-shadow: 0 -1px 0 rgba(0, 0, 0, 0.25);
    border-image: none;
    border-radius: 4px 4px 4px 4px;
    border-style: solid;
    border-width: 1px;
    box-shadow: 0 1px 0 rgba(255, 255, 255, 0.2) inset,
          0 1px 2px rgba(0, 0, 0, 0.05);
    cursor: pointer;
    display: inline-block;
    font-size: 14px;
    line-height: 20px;
    margin-bottom: 0;
    padding: 4px 12px;
    text-align: center;
    vertical-align: middle;
    position: absolute;
    right: 40px;
    bottom: 80px;
    text-decoration: none;
}
```

Now our landing page will look like this:

The landing page

The **Start now** link will send you to the chat room, but there is nothing there yet. So let us modify our routes/index.js file to serve chatroom. Add the following snippet to the end of the file:

```
exports.chatroom = function(req, res){
  res.render('chatroom', { title: 'Express Chat' });
}
```

We will also have to add the mapping to app.js:

```
app.get('/chatroom', routes.chatroom);
```

Now that we have a landing page, we are ready to add multiple rooms. We will now add support for the chat room page so that it can accept a room parameter and will connect to that room when requested. So the call to connect to enter the chat room will look like this:

```
http://localhost:3000/chatroom?room=jsconf
```

For this we need to edit our chat.js client script file:

```
var chatInfra = io.connect('/chat_infra'),
    chatCom = io.connect('/chat_com');

var roomName = decodeURI(
  (RegExp("room" + '=' + '(.+?)(&|$)').exec(location.search)
```

```
    || [, null])[1]);

if (roomName) {
    chatInfra.on('name_set', function (data) {
        chatInfra.emit('join_room', {'name':roomName});

        //EXISTING CODE
    });
}

$(function () {
    $('#setname').click(function () {
        chatInfra.emit("set_name", {name:$('#nickname').val()});
    });
});
```

The first thing is to parse the URL query to get the room name, here is how this is done:

```
var roomName = decodeURI(
    (RegExp("room" + '=' + '(.+?)(&|$)').exec(location.search)
        || [, null])[1]);
```

Here, in the preceding code, we are creating a regex to parse out the value between room= and & or to the end of the content. In the next line, we check if a room name was provided and once the user has entered the name, we will join the room.

To join the room, we emit the join_room event with roomName as a parameter. This event will be handled on the server:

```
if (roomName) {
    chatInfra.on('name_set', function (data) {
        chatInfra.emit('join_room', {'name':roomName});
```

Since we will use the room only to restrict the broadcast messages (others are anyhow sent only to the recipient's socket), this is all we need to do on the client.

Now we will edit the sockets.js file on our server to handle the join_room event on chat_infra and to change the broadcasts to send messages in the room they are meant for. Let us take a look at the changes in sockets.js:

```
var io = require('socket.io');

exports.initialize = function (server) {
    io = io.listen(server);
    var self = this;
```

```
      this.chatInfra = io.of("/chat_infra");
      this.chatInfra.on("connection", function (socket) {
        //EXISTING CODE
        });
      socket.on("join_room", function (room) {
        socket.get('nickname', function (err, nickname) {
          socket.join(room.name);
          var comSocket = self.chatCom.sockets[socket.id];
          comSocket.join(room.name);
          comSocket.room = room.name;
          socket.in(room.name).broadcast
      .emit('user_entered', {'name':nickname});
        });
      });
      });

      this.chatCom = io.of("/chat_com");
      this.chatCom.on("connection", function (socket) {
        socket.on('message', function (message) {
          message = JSON.parse(message);
          if (message.type == "userMessage") {
            socket.get('nickname', function (err, nickname) {
              message.username = nickname;
              socket.in(socket.room).broadcast.send(JSON.
      stringify(message));
              message.type = "myMessage";
              socket.send(JSON.stringify(message));
            });
          }
        });
      });
    }
```

So this brings in some minor structural changes. Since we will need to refer chatCom in chatInfra, we add them both to the current object, which is also stored as itself, so that they are accessible in the closures. In the chat_infra connection handler, we register a new event handler for join_room:

```
        socket.on("join_room", function (room) {
          socket.get('nickname', function (err, nickname) {
            socket.join(room.name);
            var comSocket = self.chatCom.sockets[socket.id];
            comSocket.join(room.name);
            comSocket.room = room.name;
            socket.in(room.name).broadcast
        .emit('user_entered', {'name':nickname});
          });
        });
```

In the handler, we are receiving the `room` object, which will in turn have the name of the room to join. Next we connect the `chat_infra` socket to the room. This is done using the `join` method of the `socket` object:

```
socket.join(room.name);
```

The `join` method takes a name string for the room. The room will be created if not present, else the socket will be connected to an existing room.

Now, once our client joins the room, it will get all the messages intended for the specific room in the `chat_infra` namespace. But, this will not be useful until we also join the room in the `chat_com` namespace. For this, we will need to obtain the `socket` object, corresponding to the current `socket` object in the `chat_com` namespace and then call the same `join` method on it:

```
var comSocket = self.chatCom.sockets[socket.id];
comSocket.join(room.name);
```

To get the corresponding `socket` object on `chat_com`, we fetch it using the current `socket` object's ID (as it will be similar) from the `sockets` array in the `chatCom` namespace object. The next line simply calls the `join` method on it. Now both have joined the room in both the namespaces. But when we receive the messages in the `chat_com` namespace, we will need the name of the room this socket is connected to. For this, we will set the `room` property on the `comSocket` object to the room it is connected to:

```
comSocket.room = room.name;
```

Now that all is set up, we will announce in the room that the user has joined:

```
socket.in(room.name).broadcast
.emit('user_entered', {'name':nickname});
});
```

As we did earlier, we still use `broadcast.emit`, but instead of calling it on the socket, we restrict it to be sent only in the room, using `in(room.name)`. Another change we make will be that of broadcasting the user messages again by restricting them to the room:

```
socket.in(socket.room).broadcast.send(JSON.stringify(message));
```

Now you can open the chat room by going to the following URL:

```
http://localhost:3000/chatroom?room=test001
```

Open this in two browser windows and log in with different names. Open another chat room in another browser window using the following URL:

```
http://localhost:3000/chatroom?room=test002
```

The messages and alerts sent only in the room test001 will be visible in the first two browsers, while the one connected to test002 will not be able to see them:

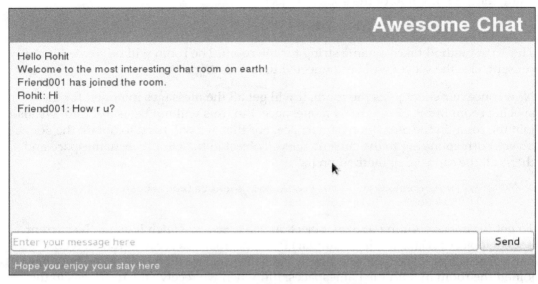

User one connected to the room test001

Here is the second user connected to the room test001:

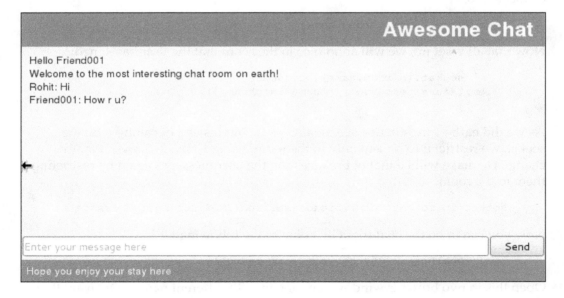

User two connected to the room test001

Here, in the following screenshot, the third user is shown connected to the room `test002`:

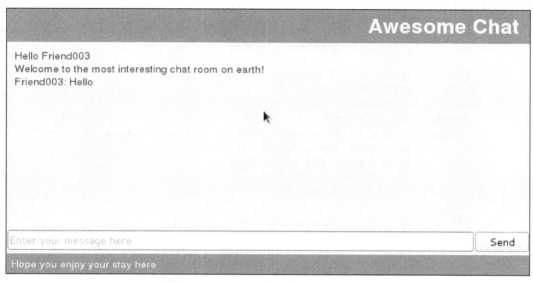

User three connected to the room test002

Listing the rooms

Now that we have support for creating multiple rooms, let us go ahead and add a page to list, join, and create new rooms. We will begin by adding a Jade view named `rooms.jade` with the following code:

```
extends layout

block append head
    script(type='text/javascript', src='/socket.io/socket.io.js')
    script(type='text/javascript', src='/javascripts/rooms.js')

block content
    section#chatrooms
      div#new_room
        span Start a new Room
        input#new_room_name(type="text")
        input#new_room_btn(type="button", value="Start")
      div#allrooms
        div#header Or join a room
        div#rooms_list
```

This view has an input box to accept a new room name and a div tag to add the list of existing rooms. We are also adding scripts for socket.io.js and a new script file for our client-side code for listing rooms, namely rooms.js. Next, create the rooms. js script file with the following code:

```
var chatInfra = io.connect('/chat_infra');

chatInfra.on("connect", function(){
    chatInfra.emit("get_rooms", {});
    chatInfra.on("rooms_list", function(rooms){
      for(var room in rooms){
        var roomDiv = '<div class="room_div"><span class="room_name">'
+ room + '</span><span class="room_users">[ '
            + rooms[room] + ' Users ] </span>'
            + '<a class="room" href="/chatroom?room=' + room
            + '">Join</a></div>';

        $('#rooms_list').append(roomDiv);
      }
    });
});

$(function(){
  $('#new_room_btn').click(function(){
      window.location = '/chatroom?room=' +
    $('#new_room_name').val();
  });
});
```

In the preceding code, we are connecting based on the chat_infra namespace, requesting the chat rooms on it, and rendering them in the view. Let us take a quick look at an important step happening here:

```
chatInfra.emit("get_rooms", {});
```

As shown in the preceding code, the first thing we do after connecting is emit an event to get_rooms. This will request the list of rooms from the server. Next, we set a listener to receive the list of rooms and render them:

```
chatInfra.on("rooms_list", function(rooms){
```

In the handler, as shown in the following code block, we are looping over the map of rooms and number of users in them and appending it to the room list:

```
for(var room in rooms){
      var roomDiv = '<div class="room_div"><span class="room_name">'
+ room + '</span><span class="room_users">[ '
          + rooms[room] + ' Users ] </span>'
```

```
                + '<a class="room" href="/chatroom?room=' + room
                + '">Join</a></div>';

        $('#rooms_list').append(roomDiv);
    }
```

Finally, we have the code to create a new room. To create a new room, all we need to do is redirect to the chat room, with the name for the new room in the URL parameters:

```
$('#new_room_btn').click(function(){
    window.location = '/chatroom?room=' +
    $('#new_room_name').val();
});
```

Next, we need to add a get_rooms handler on the server to return the list of the rooms. For this, we will add the handler on the chat_infra namespace in sockets.js:

```
this.chatInfra.on("connection", function (socket) {
    //EXISTING CODE

    socket.on("get_rooms", function(){
        var rooms = {};
        for(var room in io.sockets.manager.rooms){
            if(room.indexOf("/chat_infra/") == 0){
                var roomName = room.replace("/chat_infra/", "");
                rooms[roomName] = io.sockets.manager
            rooms[room].length;
            }
        }
        socket.emit("rooms_list", rooms);
    });
});
```

We can get the list of all the rooms using io.sockets.manager and then we can build the map expected by our client by looping over the list. In our case, we filter to get rooms only from chat_infra as they will also be created in chat_com, and we don't want duplicates. Once we have the map, we will emit it as rooms_list. Following this we will need to add the entry to our routes/index.js file, as shown here:

```
exports.rooms = function(req, res){
    res.render('rooms', { title: 'Express Chat' });
}
```

We also need to add the mapping in app.js to server rooms at /rooms:

```
app.get('/rooms', routes.rooms);
```

Finally, let us add some CSS styling for our new room's page in style.css:

```
#chatrooms{
    margin: 20px;
}

#new_room {
    font-size: 17px;
}

#new_room span{
    padding-right: 15px;
}

#allrooms #header{
    border-bottom: 1px solid;
    border-top: 1px solid;
    font-size: 17px;
    margin-bottom: 10px;
    margin-top: 16px;
    padding: 5px 0;
}

.room_div {
    border-bottom: 1px solid #CCCCCC;
    padding-bottom: 5px;
    padding-top: 12px;
}



.room_name {
    display: inline-block;
    font-weight: bold;
    width: 165px;
}

.room_div a{
    position: absolute;
    right: 40px;
}
```

Go to /rooms and create a few rooms, and then when you open the room's page in a new browser, you'll see something similar to this:

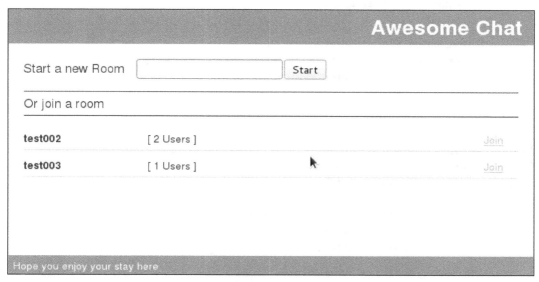

List of rooms on our chat server

Sharing the session

Now we have support for multiple rooms, but it is very clumsy to enter a nickname every time we enter a room. Let us modify our system to accept the nickname once when entering the system and use it in all the rooms.

For this, let us start by modifying the landing page to add an input box to accept a nickname and add a JavaScript file to add the logic:

```
extends layout

block append head
  script(type='text/javascript', src='/javascripts/landing.js')

block content
  section#welcome
    div Welcome
    span
      input#nickname(type="text",
    placeholder="Enter a nickname")
      a#startchat(class="btn") Login
```

Here, in the preceding code, we are adding a script entry to add `landing.js` and replacing the **Start now** button with the field to enter a name and a **Login** button. Next, let us take a look at `landing.js`:

```
$(function(){
    $('#startchat').click(function(){
        document.cookie = "nickname=" + $('#nickname').val()
                    + ";; path=/";
        window.location = "/rooms";
    });
});
```

In the previous code, we are attaching a `click` handler to the `startchat` button. In the handler, we are adding the nickname entered by the user to the cookie and redirecting the user to `/rooms`. We will be reading this cookie information while connecting the socket and then setting it on the socket. Before this cookie information can be accessed in the socket connection, we need to lay down some ground work to enable cookies in the Express.js application. For this, edit the `app.js` code by referring to the following code block:

```
var express = require('express')
  , routes = require('./routes')
  , http = require('http')
  , path = require('path')
  , connect = require('connect');

var app = express();

var sessionStore = new connect.session.MemoryStore();

app.configure(function(){
  //EXISTING CODE
  app.use(express.bodyParser());
  app.use(express.cookieParser('somesuperspecialsecrethere'));
  app.use(express.session({ key: 'express.sid',
                  store: sessionStore}));
  app.use(express.methodOverride());
  app.use(app.router);
  app.use(express.static(path.join(__dirname, 'public')));
});

//EXISTING CODE
```

The first step is to add `connect` as a dependency in the `package.json` file and the `require` keyword in `app.js`. The `connect` keyword is used to create a session store; in this case, an in-memory session store:

```
var sessionStore = new connect.session.MemoryStore();
```

We also enable the `cookieParser` middleware and the `session` module in the express application. Express' `cookieParser` middleware will take a `secret` parameter, which will be used to encrypt the cookies. The express' `session` module is initialized along with passing it the key (`express.sid` is the key for a session) and a store where the session should be maintained. In the following code, we are passing it an in-memory store, which we created in the previous step:

```
app.use(express.bodyParser());
app.use(express.cookieParser('somesuperspecialsecrethere'));
app.use(express.session({ key: 'express.sid',
                store: sessionStore}));
app.use(express.methodOverride());
app.use(app.router);
```

One important point to note about the previous code is the order of adding these two middleware components. These should be added after adding the `bodyParser` middleware and before adding the `router` middleware. If you open the browser and browse to the landing page now, you can see the cookie with the `express.sid` key in the browser's debugging tools under the **Cookies** tab. If you enter a name and click the **Enter** button, you will again see a new cookie, named after your nickname, being set:

```
var io = require('socket.io');

exports.initialize = function (server) {
  io = io.listen(server);

  io.set('authorization', function (data, accept) {
    if (data.headers.cookie) {
      data.cookie = require('cookie').parse(data.headers.cookie);
      data.sessionID = data.cookie['express.sid'].split('.')[0];
      data.nickname = data.cookie['nickname'];
    } else {
      return accept('No cookie transmitted.', false);
    }
    accept(null, true);
  });

  var self = this;
```

```
       this.chatInfra = io.of("/chat_infra");
       this.chatInfra.on("connection", function (socket) {
         socket.on("join_room", function (room) {
           var nickname = socket.handshake.nickname;
           socket.set('nickname', nickname, function () {
             socket.emit('name_set', {'name':
           socket.handshake.nickname});
             socket.send(JSON.stringify({type:'serverMessage',
               message:'Welcome to the most interesting ' +
                   'chat room on earth!'}));
             socket.join(room.name);
             var comSocket = self.chatCom.sockets[socket.id];
             comSocket.join(room.name);
             comSocket.room = room.name;
             socket.in(room.name).broadcast.emit('user_entered',
                       {'name':nickname});
           });
         });

         //EXISTING CODE
       }
```

The first change in the preceding code block introduces us to a new feature in socket. io; this change is shown in the following highlighted code block:

```
   io.set('authorization', function (data, accept) {
     if (data.headers.cookie) {
       data.cookie = require('cookie').parse(data.headers.cookie);
       data.sessionID = data.cookie['express.sid'].split('.')[0];
       data.nickname = data.cookie['nickname'];
     } else {
       return accept('No cookie transmitted.', false);
     }
     accept(null, true);
   });
```

In this code snippet, we are setting an authorization method for the socket. This method will get two parameters, the data that contains all the HTTP request information and the accept method callback. The authorization method is called when a socket.io connection is requested but before it is established.

We can use this method for actually performing an authorization, but in our case we will just use it to get the nickname from the cookies, as this is the only socket.io method that will have the HTTP data available with it.

We are reading the cookie headers from the HTTP data and are parsing it using the cookie module's parse method. From the cookie, we are extracting the sessionID value and the nickname and setting it to the data object. This object is available on the socket as the handshake property. Finally, we will call the accept callback, which accepts two parameters, first a message and another a Boolean variable, indicating whether the authorization was successful or not.

We will remove the set_name handler, as this handler need not be called because we already have the name with us. We will move the logic from the set_name handler to the join_room handler:

```
socket.on("join_room", function (room) {
  var nickname = socket.handshake.nickname;
  socket.set('nickname', nickname, function () {
    socket.emit('name_set', {'name': nickname});
    socket.send(JSON.stringify({type:'serverMessage',
      message:'Welcome to the most interesting ' +
        'chat room on earth!'}));
    socket.join(room.name);
    var comSocket = self.chatCom.sockets[socket.id];
    comSocket.join(room.name);
    comSocket.room = room.name;
    socket.in(room.name).broadcast.emit('user_entered',
               {'name':nickname});
  });
});
```

In the join_room handler, we will fetch the nickname from the socket.handshake map and set it as a property on the socket. On setting the nickname property, we will still trigger the name_set event so as to keep the changes on the client to a minimum:

```
var chatInfra = io.connect('/chat_infra'),
    chatCom = io.connect('/chat_com');

var roomName = decodeURI((RegExp("room" + '=' + '(.+?)(&|$)').
exec(location.search) || [, null])[1]);

if (roomName) {
  chatInfra.emit('join_room', {'name':roomName});

  chatInfra.on('name_set', function (data) {
  //EXISTING CODE
  });
}
```

As the `join_room` handler is the initializer for the room on the server, we will take it out of the `name_set` handler and directly call it during the page load. The rest of the code remains as is.

To try this code, you will have to open two different browsers or browsers in different incognito sessions as the cookies/sessions will be shared for the same browser.

Summary

In this chapter, we saw how to set data for a session, how to work with namespaces and rooms, and how to integrate with the express sessions. Here we have completed a good and working chat system. It will be a nice exercise for you to build more functionality in this, based on the concepts we learned here. Some interesting features to build can be user exist alert, user list for the rooms, private chats, and so on. In the next chapter, we will take a look at the socket.io protocol and understand its workings.

5

The Socket.IO Protocol

Socket.io provides a very simple API that is easy to use but exposes a lot of functionality. Moreover, this functionality works uniformly across browsers and the various transport mechanisms provided by socket.io. To achieve this, a socket.io client and server do a lot of work in the background. In this chapter, we will examine and try to understand the communication in socket.io as well as some socket.io internals.

Why do we need another protocol?

The first question to people familiar with WebSocket is, why do we need another protocol when we already have WebSocket? The answer is twofold; socket.io works in a uniform manner across browsers (dating back to Internet Explorer 6), and socket.io provides a much richer API.

The WebSocket specification is still under development and is not supported on many of the browsers that are in use. In fact, any version of Internet Explorer prior to IE10 doesn't have support for WebSocket. There are still many people out there using old browsers that don't support WebSocket.

Another problem for WebSocket is firewalls and proxies. Most of the firewalls block any communication (apart from standard HTTP 1.0/1.1), and may not allow a WebSocket connection to be established. The same applies to most proxy servers.

So, if we decide to use just the WebSocket protocol, we have to understand that there will be many people who may not be able to use our application.

Contrary to this, when we build our application using socket.io, the people who can use WebSocket will continue using it, but those who can't will fall back on the next best available transport mechanism and then the next and so on, until they find one that works in the browser, even through the firewalls and proxies, all the way down to iframes (which is rarely used). The default order is as follows:

- WebSocket
- FlashSocket
- XHR long polling
- XHR multipart streaming
- XHR polling
- JSONP polling
- iframe

It's also worth noting that using JSONP polling, socket.io provides support for cross-domain communication without the need for any special configuration on the server or any special code on the client.

Now, let us take a look at the differences in the API. For this, we will see only the JavaScript client-side API, as any server will have its own implementation and API depending on the programming language used.

The WebSocket API

Let us begin by taking a quick look at a code snippet showing the skeleton of a WebSocket client:

```
<script>
  var socket = new WebSocket('ws://localhost:8080');

  socket.onopen = function(event) {
    socket.send('Client socket connected');
  };

  socket.onmessage = function(event) {
    console.log('Client received a message', event);
  };

  socket.onclose = function(event) {
    console.log('Client socket disconnected', event);
  };

  //socket.close()
</script>
```

The first step, as can be seen in the previous code snippet, is to create a new instance of WebSocket; in this, we have to pass the URI for the WebSocket server. This URI, like any other, has a part that specifies the protocol, which in this case can be either `ws` (unsecured) or `wss` (secured); the server address (the server's IP address or valid domain name); and finally, the port.

Ideally, we also need to check if WebSocket is supported on the browser that the user has, but I have skipped that part to focus on the API.

Following the creation of the WebSocket object, we can attach event handlers to it. There are three events exposed by WebSocket, with their corresponding event handlers:

- `open`: The `onopen` event handler
- `message`: The `onmessage` event handler
- `close`: The `onclose` event handler

As is evident by their names, these handlers will be called on the opening of a socket connection, when there is a new message on the socket, and on closing the socket connection, respectively.

For every event, the client receives the event data. In case the event is a message, it contains that message along with other data. The WebSocket client doesn't try to interpret the message or its type, that is to say, it treats all messages as plain text and it is left to the application to interpret and understand it. Also, there is no mention of the namespacing of messages or the multiplexing of socket connections.

If you see the `onopen` handler, you will notice the `send` method, which is used by the client to send messages. Again, it can send only plain text, so you have to take care of serialization and deserialization.

Finally, we have the `close` method, which, as the name suggests, can be used to close the socket connection from the client.

The Socket.IO API

Let us see the same code using socket.io:

```
<script>
  var socket = io.connect('http://localhost:8080');

  socket.on('connect', function() {
    socket.send('Client socket connected');
  });
```

```
socket.on('message', function(data) {
  console.log('Received a message from the server!',data);
});

socket.on('disconnect', function() {
  console.log('The client socket disconnected!');
});

</script>
```

The above code snippet looks similar to the one with WebSockets and, not surprisingly, does the same work as the previous code. However, there are some minor changes: instead of using onopen, onmessage, and onclose, we use socket. io's on method to attach the handlers. The advantage is that when we use socket.io's custom events functionality, the API to handle the event remains the same.

As we have already seen, you can emit a new event using the following line of code:

```
socket.emit("myevent", {"eventData": "..."});
```

And then receive it using the following:

```
socket.on("myevent", function(event){...});
```

As you can see, in this case, we are passing a JSON object for the data; socket.io will take care of serializing and deserializing it for us.

Moreover, socket.io provides support for namespacing of messages, multiplexing of connections, disconnection detection, reconnection, and an API to broadcast messages to all clients.

Considering everything covered in this section, it is not difficult to conclude that socket.io will need its own protocol and mechanism to work.

The Socket.IO socket

The socket.io socket emulates a network socket over different transport mechanisms. Just as any other socket, it has various stages in its lifecycle, depending on the status of the connection. These are as follows:

* connecting
* connected
* disconnecting
* disconnected

The socket is established when the client sends a connection request to the server and a handshake is initiated.

Once the handshake is complete, a connection is opened using the transport negotiated during the handshake, and the state of the socket is set to *connected*.

To check the liveliness of the socket depending on the server configuration, the server may require heartbeat messages to be sent from the client to the server in regular intervals. In the absence of such a message, or the failure of the underlying transport, the socket will be disconnected.

In this case, the client will initiate a reconnect. If the connection is restored within the connection termination time or the timeout agreed at the time of the handshake, the buffered messages are sent across. In case the connection is not restored, the client will start a new connection request, beginning with a new handshake.

Also, optionally, to ensure message delivery over the socket, we can make it compulsory for the socket to acknowledge the message delivery.

The socket is terminated when the `close` method is called on either the client or the server.

The Socket.IO connection

The socket.io connection begins with the handshake. This makes the handshake a special part of the protocol. Apart from the handshake, all the other events and messages in the protocol are transferred over the socket.

Socket.io is intended for use with web applications, and therefore it is assumed that these applications will always be able to use HTTP. It is because of this reasoning that the socket.io handshake takes place over HTTP.

To initiate the connection and hence perform the handshake, the client performs a `POST` request on the handshake URI (built from the URI passed to the `connect` method). Let us take the same socket.io connection URI and try to understand its various parts. Let us say that the URI is as follows:

```
http://myhost.com:8080/socket.io/1/
```

Let us break down and understand this URI.

`http` is the protocol being used. We can set it to use `https`, using `https` in the client's `connect` method.

`myhost.com` again comes from the `connect` method and is the name or IP address of the host you want to connect to. The default is `localhost`.

`8080` is the port over which your server is listening. This is also passed to the `connect` method when we are invoking it. The default is `80`.

`socket.io` is the namespace that handles all the connect requests.

`1` is the socket.io protocol version number.

The server can respond to this in one of these three ways:

- `200 OK` – This will be the server's response when the handshake is successful. In addition to the status, the body of the response should be a colon-separated list of the session ID given to this connection, the heartbeat timeout, the connection closing timeout, and the list of supported transports separated by commas. A sample response body looks like this:

  `8749dke9387:20:10:websocket,flashsocket,xhr-polling`

- `401 Unauthorized` – This will be the response from the server in case the authorization handler fails to authorize the client. As we saw in the previous chapter, this is the handler we attach to the `authorize` event on the server, and it uses the connection and cookie information to authorize the user.

- `503 Service Unavailable` – When the server has any other reason, including errors, to deny service to the client.

If the handshake is successful, based on the transports provided by the server and the one supported by the client the socket.io client will start communicating with the server on a particular URI. This URI has the form `[scheme]://[host]/ [namespace]/[version]/[transportId]/[sessionId]`.

- `[scheme]` is the protocol the client will be using to communicate. In the case of WebSockets, this is either `ws` or `wss`, while in the case of XHR, it is either `http` or `https`.

- `[host]` is the server name or IP Address.

- `[namespace]` is the socket.io namespace we want to send the message to.

- `[version]` is the version of the socket.io protocol that we are using, currently `1`.

- `[transportId]` is the the name of the transport mechanism chosen for the communication.

- `[sessionId]` is the session ID given to the client by the server during the handshake.

In the case of bidirectional transport, such as WebSocket, the connection opened at this URI will be used to send and receive messages.

For unidirectional transports such as XHR long polling, the client will perform a GET request on this URI, which the server will keep on hold till it has some data to send, while the client will perform a POST request on this URI whenever it has to send a message or an event to the server.

Socket.IO messages

Once the transport's connection is established, all the communication between the client and server happens using messaging over the socket. The messages need to be encoded in the format specified by socket.io.

This format enables socket.io to determine the type of the message and the data sent in the message, and some metadata useful for operation. The message format is [type] : [id ('+')] : [endpoint] (: [data]).

- type is a single digit integer, specifying what type of message it is.
- id is the message ID, which is an incremental integer; it is used for ACKs. It is optional.
- The + sign, if present, tells socket.io not to handle the ACKs, as the application intends to handle it.
- endpoint is the socket endpoint that the message is intended to be delivered to. This is optional and is used when multiplexing the socket for namespacing. If omitted, the message will be sent to the default socket.
- data is the associated data to be delivered to the socket. In the case of messages, it is treated as plain text, while in the case of events, it will be parsed as JSON.

In the coming section, we will see what the types of messages are.

Disconnect (0)

When the type is zero (0), the message is a disconnect signal. This will tell socket.io to close the connection and the mentioned socket. If the endpoint is not specified, the message will be sent to the default socket, which will cause the whole socket to be closed and all the endpoints on that socket will be terminated. For example:

- Message: 0 – The result is that the socket is closed and all the connections/endpoints are terminated.
- Message: 0::/endpoint – The socket connection to /endpoint will be closed and no messages can be sent to or from that endpoint. Other endpoints will continue to operate.

Connect (1)

This message is only used for multiplexing, and is sent from the client to the server to open a new connection. Thus, this message must always have an endpoint. The first (default) socket connection is established by the handshake explained earlier. The endpoint may be followed by query parameters in a URL query format. If the connection is successful, the server will echo the same message, else the server can send an error message. For example:

- Message: `1::/endpoint` – Requests the server to open a multiplexed socket to the endpoint.

- Message: `0::/endpoint?param=one` – Requests the server to open a multiplexed socket to the endpoint, passing a parameter called `param` with the value `one`.

Heartbeat (2)

This is the heartbeat message. It must be sent from the client to the server within the timeout negotiated during the handshake. The server will reply with a heartbeat message too. In this case, we don't have an endpoint and nor is any other information required. This is because it serves the whole socket. For example:

- Message: `2` – Sends a heartbeat message to the other end.

Message (3)

This is the message sent over the socket. In the API, this message will be sent when you are using `socket.send`, and will result in a message event on the receiving end. This message will carry data, treating it as plain text. For example:

- Message: `3:1::Some message` – This will send a message to the other end, where the message event handler will be triggered with the `Some message` message in the event data.

- Message: `3:1:/endpoint:Some message` – Again, the message will be sent to other end of the socket, but on the multiplexed endpoint.

JSON message (4)

This is similar to sending the message, but in this case the message has to be serialized using JSON, and it will be parsed at the other end before being sent to the handler. In version 0.6, this was done using the same API as `send()` for message, just passing a JSON message instead of a string message. But since this introduces a performance penalty over sending plain text from version 0.7 onwards, we have to use the `json` flag to send a JSON message; for example, `socket.json.send`. For example:

- Message: `4:1::{"some":"content"}` – Sends the JSON message to the other end of the socket.

Event (5)

The Event message is a special kind of JSON message that is used to send events over the socket. In events, the data payload is of the form `{"name":"eventName", "args":{"some":"content"}}`.

Here, `name` is the name of the event and `args` are the parameters to be sent to the handler. The `socket.emit` call is used to send events in the applications.

The following event names are reserved and cannot be used in applications:

- `message`
- `connect`
- `disconnect`
- `open`
- `close`
- `error`
- `retry`
- `reconnect`

For example:

- Message: `5:1::{"name": "myEvent", "args":{"some": "data"}}` – The result is that the event will be sent to the other end and the appropriate event handler will be invoked, passing the args to it.

ACK (6)

The acknowledgment (ACK) message will be sent when the message is received, with ACK request enabled; or, it can be sent out by the application. The data section in the ACK message can be the message ID for the message that is being acknowledged. If the message ID is followed by + and additional data, it is treated as an event packet. For example:

- Message: `6:::1` – Sends an acknowledgment for the receipt of a message with ID `1`.

- Message: `6:::1+["A", "B"]` – This will send an acknowledgment for the message along with the data.

Error (7)

This is sent by the server in case there's an error, such as failure during the processing of a `connect` request to an endpoint. The data section of this message will contain the error message and, optionally, advice, separated by the + sign. For example:

- Message: `7:::Unauthorized` – The result is that the error will be sent to the client.

NOOP (8)

This message implies no operation, and is used to close a poll after the polling times out.

Summary

In this chapter, we saw the communication mechanism for the socket.io server and client. Understanding the working and the message formats, helps us in debugging the issues we face during the development of socket.io applications.

In the next chapter we will learn to deploy and scale socket.io applications in production. Also, we will get a few tips on how to minimize our troubles on the production server.

6
Deploying and Scaling

Running our application on the local server is fine, but making a web application really useful requires deploying it to a public server and making it accessible to others. To run our chat server application on Node.js, along with using protocols such as WebSocket, requires some special considerations. In this chapter, we will take a look at the following:

- Things to consider while deploying our application
- Recommendations for a production-ready deployment
- Reason why scaling of socket.io applications is different than other web applications
- How we can scale our chat application

The production environment

The first thing we should do before running an application on a production server is to set the environment to production. Every modern server or framework has separate development and production modes and so does node. In fact, in node you can set the environment to any name and then have different configurations for that name in your code. To set the environment our node server runs in, we set an environment variable NODE_ENV to the environment we want to run node in. So, to run node in the production environment, we use the following line:

```
$ export NODE_ENV=production
```

And then run your node application. In *Chapter 2, Getting Started with Node.js*, we saw how the first argument in `app.configure` is the environment variable we need to configure for:

```
app.configure('development', function(){
  app.use(express.errorHandler());
});
```

In this snippet we are setting the application to activate `express.errorHandler` in the `development` environment, which is the default environment. If we have set `NODE_ENV` to `production`, `express.errorHandler` will not be used.

Running the application

Running the application on the command line using node, like we have been doing until now, works during development; but on a production server where we connect remotely, it is generally not feasible or advisable to keep the console running. There are two ways to handle this, either we run node as a background process redirecting all console output to a file or we run it in a persistent console, to which we can reconnect, using `screen` or `byobu`.

To run node as a background process, like any other process on Linux, we will use the `&` operator and to make sure that it keeps running even after we log out, we will use `nohup`:

```
$ nohup npm start 2>&1 >> npmout.log &
```

The preceding command will redirect the `stdout` and `stderr` commands to `npmout.log` and will put the npm process in the background.

Another option is to run node on a long-lasting console, using utilities such as `screen` or `byobu`. To use this, start `screen` and then run your application, as shown here:

```
$ screen
```

```
$ npm start
```

Now we can detach from this screen by using *Ctrl +a* and then hitting *d*. This will drop us to the default shell. We can then disconnect. When we connect back to the server, to see the server output, we can attach back to the screen by using the following command:

```
$ screen -r
```

Keeping it running

Not only do we want the application to run when we log out, we want our application to keep running reliably. The production servers are not frequently restarted, and in general we will like to ensure that they come back up as soon as possible when there is a crash, a failure, or an error. For node, generally it means restarting the process as soon as it fails. There are many ways to keep the node server running. In this section we will see two of them:

* Monit
* Forever

Here is how Monit is described on its website (`http://mmonit.com/monit/`):

Monit is a free open source utility for managing and monitoring processes, programs, files, directories, and filesystems on a UNIX system. Monit conducts automatic maintenance and repair and can execute meaningful causal actions in error situations.

Let us begin with installing Monit. On RPM-based or Yum-based systems such as RHEL, Fedora, or CentOS, you can install it using the `yum` command, as shown here:

```
$ sudo yum install monit
```

Or on a Debian- or apt-get-based system, you can install Monit using `apt-get`:

```
$ apt-get install monit
```

For other systems, you can check the installation instructions at the Monit website.

Once Monit is installed, we can configure it to manage our node application. For this, we will create a configuration file (in our case we will call it `awesome-chat`) in `/etc/monit.d/` or `/etc/monit/conf.d/`, depending on your Monit installation:

```
check host objdump with address 127.0.0.1
    start program = "/bin/sh -c \
    'NODE_ENV=production \
    node /opt/node_apps/awesome-chat/app.js 2>&1 \
    >> /var/log/awesome-chat.log'"
        as uid nobody and gid nobody
    stop program  = "/usr/bin/pkill -f \
    'node /opt/node_apps/awesome-chat/app.js'"
    if failed port 3000 protocol HTTP
        request /
        with timeout 10 seconds
        then restart
```

In this file, you should notice the highlighted section. We are emphasizing the program or more importantly, the commands to start/stop our application and then finally configuring Monit to restart the application in case of a failure. This is detected by sending an HTTP request to fetch the page at port 3000.

That is it; we can start our application with the following command:

```
$ monit start awesome-chat
```

And stop it with the following code:

```
$ monit stop awesome-chat
```

In case of a crash, Monit will take care of restarting the application.

Monit can be used to run and watch any daemon service. It also has a web interface in case you want to check the status, which by default runs on port 2812. You can learn more about Monit on its website and in its manual online.

Another, more node-specific way to keep our server up and running is **Forever** (https://github.com/nodejitsu/forever). Forever describes itself as:

> *A simple CLI tool for ensuring that a given script runs continuously.*

And that's what is does. Given your node application script, Forever will start it and make sure it keeps running continuously. Since Forever itself is a node application, we will use npm to install it:

```
$ sudo npm install forever -g
```

Now, to start the application with Forever, it is just a matter of executing the app.js file with forever. Just run the following command:

```
$ forever start app.js
```

We can see the list of applications running forever with the following command:

```
$ forever list
  0 app.js [ 24597, 24596 ]
```

To stop the application, use the forever stop command:

```
$ forever stop 0
```

Visit Forever's github page for understanding more about Forever and its workings.

There are several other tools on *nix systems to make node run as a daemon. Few of them are as follows:

- Upstart (`http://upstart.ubuntu.com/`)
- Supervisord (`http://supervisord.org/`)
- Daemontools (`http://cr.yp.to/daemontools.html`)

Scaling

Now that we have made sure that our application will keep running and also will restart from failures, it's time we start looking at ways to handle millions of users flocking to our chat room. To begin with this, the first step is to put up a load-balancer proxy in front of our server. There are lots of options in this, we can use the Apache HTTP server, Nginx, and so on. All these servers work very well with balancing traditional HTTP traffic, but still have some time to catch up to work with WebSockets. So we will use a server that works on load-balancing TCP/IP itself. This is **HAProxy** (`http://haproxy.1wt.eu/`). This is how HAProxy is described in its official website:

> *HAProxy is a free, very fast and reliable solution offering high availability, load balancing, and proxying for TCP and HTTP-based applications. It is particularly suited for web sites crawling under very high loads while needing persistence or Layer7 processing. Supporting tens of thousands of connections is clearly realistic with today's hardware.*

HAProxy works with frontends and backends. These are configured using the HAProxy configuration file present at `/etc/haproxy/haproxy.cfg`. The following file creates a frontend listener at port `80` and forwards it to a single server at `3000`:

```
global
  maxconn 4096

defaults
  environment http

frontend all 0.0.0.0:80
  default_backend www_Node.js

backend www_Node.js
  environment http
  option forwardfor
  server Node.js 127.0.0.1:3000 weight 1 maxconn 10000 check
```

In this file, we are defining a frontend listener at `0.0.0.0:80` with the default `www_Node.js` backend listening at `3000` on the same `127.0.0.1` server.

But this configuration is not ready to handle WebSockets. To support and handle WebSockets, refer to the following code block:

```
global
  maxconn 4096

defaults
  environment http

frontend all 0.0.0.0:80
  timeout client 86400000
  default_backend www_Node.js
  acl is_websocket hdr(upgrade) -i websocket
  acl is_websocket hdr_beg(host) -i ws

  use_backend www_Node.js if is_websocket

backend www_Node.js
  environment http
  option forwardfor
  timeout server 86400000
  timeout connect 4000
  server Node.js 127.0.0.1:3000 weight 1 maxconn 10000 check
```

The first thing we did was to increase the client timeout value, so the client connection doesn't drop off if there is a long inactivity from the client. The `acl` lines of code instruct HAProxy to understand and check when we get a `websocket` request.

By using the `use_backend` instruction, we configure HAProxy to use the `www_Node.js` backend to handle the `websocket` request. This is useful when you want to serve your static pages from any server, such as Apache HTTP, and want to use node exclusively to handle socket.io.

Now we come to the part where we would like the request to be handled by more than one node server/process. To do this, first we will tell the proxy to round robin the requests by adding the following instruction to the backend:

```
balance roundrobin
```

Then we will add more server entries to the backend:

```
server Node.js 127.0.0.1:4000 weight 1 maxconn 10000 check
server Node.js 192.168.1.101:3000 weight 1 maxconn 10000 check
```

Here we are adding two new node instances: one is a new process listening on port 4000 on the same server, while the other one is running on another server, which is accessible to the load-balancer at 192.168.1.101 on port 3000.

We are done configuring the servers and the incoming requests will now be routed between the three node instances that we have configured.

The node cluster

Node now comes with its own completely rewritten cluster module. Cluster allows node to start multiple processes behind the cluster frontend and monitors and manages them. We will take a quick look at how to make an application cluster with this module, but note that this is only for creating multiple processes and we must still set up a tool to monitor the cluster master and also a proxy to forward requests to the node server.

Let us see how we can use the cluster module. The best part about the cluster module is you don't need to actually change your application. Cluster will run a master instance, and we can start multiple instances of our application and they will all listen to a shared port.

Here is the script that we can use for clustering the app.js file:

```
var cluster = require('cluster');

if (cluster.isMaster) {
  var noOfWorkers =
          process.env.NODE_WORKERS || require('os').cpus().length;
  while(workers.length < noOfWorkers) {
    cluster.fork();
  }
} else {
  require('./app.js');
}
```

So, what's happening here? The first thing we do is use require on the cluster module. In the next line, we are checking whether the instance that is started is the master process or the worker.

If it is the master process, we check if the NODE_WORKERS environment variable is set, else we get the number of processors available on the system our server is running on. To set the NODE_WORKERS environment variable, you can run the following:

```
$ export NODE_WORKERS=2
```

The previous command will tell the cluster to start two nodes.

Now, in the loop, we call `fork` on the cluster. This calls `child_process.fork` so that the master and the started workers can communicate via IPC.

When the cluster process is run from `fork`, `cluster.isMaster` is false and so our `app.js` script is in the current worker process.

In our application, when we call `server.listen(3000)`, the worker serializes this and sends over the request to the server, the server checks if it already is listening on that port, and returns the handle for the listener, if it is present. Else, the server starts listening on the port and passes on the handle to the newly created listener.

Since all our workers request to listen on port `3000`, the server will start listening on the port when the first worker starts and will pass on the same handler to all the workers. When a request comes in, it will be handled by any worker that can take it up and process it.

Since our monitoring tool (Monit or Forever, or others) will now be monitoring only the master process, it becomes the master's responsibility to monitor the workers. This means that the cluster should restart any worker that happens to die. We will do this, by adding the following event handler in the master process:

```
cluster.on('exit', function (worker, code, signal){
  var exitCode = worker.process.exitCode;
  console.log('worker ' + worker.process.pid +
                          ' died ('+exitCode+'). restarting...');
  cluster.workers[worker.id].delete();
  cluster.fork();
});
```

Monitoring of the process is done by listening to the `exit` event on the socket. This is the event that will be triggered when any worker dies. The event handler will get the worker, its exit code, and the signal that caused the process to be killed. In the handler, we log the death and we start a new worker process using `cluster.fork()`.

Now we can start the new clustered application; we'll run `cluster.js` instead of `app.js`. So change the `start` script in `package.json` to run `cluster.js`:

```
"scripts": {
  "start": "node cluster",
}
```

And then run the application with npm.

```
npm start
```

This will start the application and everything will look just as it was. But when you start using it, you'll notice that there are errors while trying to connect to a room, or while sending messages. These errors are because we are using an in-memory store for our Express.js sessions and socket.io uses an in-memory store to store and transfer all the messages.

Scaling up the application

In the previous section we saw how we can cluster a Node.js app and how it remains restricted due to our application mechanisms. In its current state, the application uses an in-memory store to keep the session data. This store is local to the Node. js instance and so won't be accessible in any another clustered instance. Also, the data will be lost in a Node.js instance restart. So, what we need is a way to store the session in a persistent store. Also, we want to configure socket.io such that all its instances use a shared pub-sub and data store. The Connect framework has an extension mechanism so a new store can be plugged in, and there is one store that is persistent as well as excels at pub-sub. It is the **Redis Session Store**.

Redis (http://redis.io/) is a high performance, distributed, open source key-value store that can also be used as a queue. We will use Redis and corresponding Redis stores to provide a reliable, distributed, and shared store and pub-sub queue. Please check out the instructions to install the Redis server on your operating system and start it up.

Let's make a few changes to our chat application, beginning with package.json:

```
"connect-redis":"*",
"redis":"*"
```

This will add support for the Connect/Express.js Redis store and the Redis connection client. Let's first get Express.js to use Redis; to do so, edit app.js by referring to the following code snippet:

```
var express = require('express')
  , routes = require('./routes')
  , http = require('http')
  , path = require('path')
  , connect = require('connect')
  , RedisStore = require('connect-redis')(express);

var app = express();

var sessionStore = new RedisStore();

//Existing Code
```

So the two changes we make here are pulling in the Redis session store and then we can replace the session store to be an instance of `RedisStore`. That's all that is needed to get Express running using the Redis store.

The next thing we need to do is get socket.io using Redis. So, let us edit `socket.js`:

```
var io = require('socket.io')
  , redis = require('redis')
  , RedisStore = require('socket.io/lib/stores/redis')
  , pub     = redis.createClient()
  , sub     = redis.createClient()
  , client = redis.createClient();

exports.initialize = function (server) {
  io = io.listen(server);

  io.set('store', new RedisStore({
      redisPub : pub
    , redisSub : sub
    , redisClient : client
  }));

  //Existing Code
}
```

The first thing in the preceding code snippet that we are doing is `require ('redis')`, which provides the client and `redisStore` from socket.io, which provides redis backed for socket.io. Then we create three different Redis clients to use for pub-sub and the data store:

```
  io.set('store', new RedisStore({
      redisPub : pub
    , redisSub : sub
    , redisClient : client
  }));
```

In the previous code snippet, we configure socket.io to use Redis for the queue and data store. And we are ready to go! Now run the application again using the following command:

```
npm start
```

Tips for node in production

Here are some tips to help us execute node in production:

1. Run the server in the `production` environment.

2. Never expose the node application directly on the Internet; always use a proxy. Servers such as Apache HTTP, Nginx, and HAProxy have been hardened and made robust over the years in production to make them secure against various kinds of attacks, especially DOS and DDOS. Node is new; it may become stable over time but today it is not recommended to be put directly on the front.

3. Never run node as root. Well, that is the advice for any application server, and it applies to node too. If we run node as root, there are chances of hackers gaining root access or running some harmful code as root. So, never ever run it as root!

4. Always run more than one node process. Node is a single-threaded, single-process application server. An error in the application can bring the server down. So, always have more than one process for reliability. Also, thinking in terms of 1+ processes keeps us ready for scaling out when the need comes.

5. Always use a monitor. Monit, Forever, Upstart pick one you like, but always use it. Better safe than sorry.

6. Never use `MemoryStore` in `production`; `MemoryStore` is for the `development` environment; I recommend using `RedisStore` even in `development`.

7. Log all errors. Everything runs fine until it doesn't! And when something goes wrong, logs are your best friend. Try to catch exceptions as close to the cause as possible and log all the relevant information in the context. Don't just log some error message, log all the relevant objects.

8. Never block unless there is no alternative. Node runs on an event loop, and blocking for one request will cause unwanted overheads and degrade performance for all requests.

9. Always keep your server, node, and all dependency modules up-to-date.

Summary

In this section, we saw the work involved in putting our application to production. We must remember that these are not the only ways to do it. For every task we did, there are many other ways of doing them, and there is no one solution that fits all scenarios. But now that we know what is expected out of a `production` environment, we can research the options and choose one according to our requirements.

Socket.IO Quick Reference

In this appendix we will take a look at the APIs provided by socket.io. The intention is to have a cursory glance through all the APIs so we know if there is a function that can help us while we are working. Socket.io is under active development and the APIs themselves are subject to change. Although the documented methods may not change, there are always new functions and features being added to socket.io. So always check with the socket.io website and wiki for the availability of a function that does what you want.

The server

As we already know by now, socket.io provides libraries to be used both in the server and the client. Let's first see the APIs provided for the server.

Instantiating socket

The `socket.io` module is instantiated, just like any other node module, by using `require` to import the module:

```
var io = require('socket.io');
```

Starting Socket.IO

The socket.io server component is started by using the `listen` method, which attaches the socket.io to the node HTTP server:

```
var sio = io.listen(<server>)
```

Here, `server` is the instance of the node HTTP server.

Listening to events

The event handlers are attached to socket using the on method. The on method takes the event name and the callback/handler function as parameters:

```
sio.on(<event>, function(eventData){
  //DO SOMETHING
});
```

Here, event is the name of the event and eventData represents the event-specific data passed to the handler when it is invoked.

Emitting an event

We use the emit method to trigger an event. This event will be handled on the client:

```
socket.emit(<event>, <event_data>, ack_callback);
```

Here, event is the name of the event to trigger, event_data is the event data as a JSON object, and ack_callback is the optional callback function that is invoked on the successful receipt of the event on the client.

Sending a message

The send method is used to send a message to the client:

```
socket.send(<message>, ack_callback);
```

Where message is the message that will be sent to the client and ack_callback is the optional callback function that is invoked on the successful receipt of the message on the client.

Sending a JSON message

A JSON message can be sent by using the json flag before the send method:

```
socket.json.send(<message>, ack_callback);
```

Here, message is the message that will be sent to the client and ack_callback is the optional callback function that is invoked on the successful receipt of the message on the client.

Broadcasting a message/event

A message or an event can be broadcasted to all the connected sockets using the `broadcast` flag:

```
socket.broadcast.emit(<event>, <event_data>);
```

Here, `event` is the name of event to emit and `event_data` is the JSON data that will be sent with the event. The following line of code shows how to broadcast a message:

```
socket.broadcast.send(<message>);
```

Here, `message` is the message that will be sent to the client and `ack_callback` is the optional callback function that is invoked on the successful receipt of the message on the client.

Sending a volatile message

Sometimes the message being sent is not important and can be ignored if not delivered. So these methods need not be queued or attempted to be redelivered. This is done with the `volatile` flag:

```
socket.volatile.send(<message>);
```

Here, `message` is the message that will be sent to the client and `ack_callback` is the optional callback function that is invoked on the successful receipt of the message on the client.

Storing socket data

We can call the `set` method on the socket to store some data on the socket. This is an asynchronous method call and takes a key, value, and a callback function:

```
socket.set(<key>, <value>, function(){
  //DO SOMETHING
});
```

Here, `key` is the key name for this data and `value` is the value to store.

Getting the socket data

We use the `get` method to fetch the value stored on a socket. This is an asynchronous method and takes a key and a callback function, which will get the value:

```
socket.get(<key>, function(value){
  //DO SOMETHING
});
```

Here, `key` is the key of the data to fetch and `value` is the value if stored with the socket. This will be `null` if the value is not stored.

Restricting to a namespace

We can multiplex the socket and restrict messages/events to a namespace by using the `of` method. This method returns a socket, which can be used as any other socket, but the messages will be restricted to only the clients connected to this namespace:

```
var namespace_socket = socket.of(<namespace>);
```

Here, `namespace` is the namespace we want to restrict the socket to.

Joining a room

We use the `join` method of `socket` to join a room. It will create a new room if one doesn't already exist:

```
socket.join(<room>);
```

Here, `room` is the name of the room to join.

Broadcasting messages/events in a room

We can send messages to all the connected clients in the room by using the `in` flag with `broadcast`:

```
socket.broadcast.in(<room>).send(<message>);
socket.broadcast.in(<room>).emit(<event>, <event_data>);
```

Here, `room` is the room to send the message in, `message` is the message to send, `event` is the event to emit, and `event_data` is the data to be sent with the event.

Leaving a room

The `leave` method is used to leave a room. We don't need to do this explicitly if the socket is exiting. Also, an empty room will automatically be destroyed:

```
socket.leave(<room>);
```

Here, `room` is the room to exit from.

Changing the configuration

Socket.io is configured using the `set` method in the `configure` method's callback handler:

```
io.configure('environment', function () {
  io.set(<property>, <value>);
});
```

Here, `environment` is the optional environment in which this configuration will be used, `property` is the property to be set, and `value` is the value for the property.

Server events

We will discuss some server-related events in this section.

connection

This event is fired when an initial connection with a client is established:

```
io.sockets.on('connection', function(socket) {})
```

Here, `socket` is used in further communication with the client.

message

The `message` event is emitted when a message sent with `socket.send` is received:

```
socket.on('message', function(<message>, <ack_callback>) {})
```

Here, `message` is the message sent and `ack_callback` is an optional acknowledgment function.

disconnect

This event is fired when the socket disconnects:

```
socket.on('disconnect', function() {})
```

The client

In this section we will get to know the client APIs.

Connecting to a socket

We connect to a socket using the `connect` method on the `io` object in the client:

```
var socket = io.connect(<uri>);
```

Here, `uri` is the server URI to connect to. It can be absolute or relative. If it is other than /, or an absolute equivalent of that, it will connect to the namespace.

Listening to events

We can attach event handlers to a socket using the `on` method:

```
socket.on(<event>, function(event_data, ack_callback){});
```

Here, `event` is the event to listen for, `event_data` is the data for the event, and `ack_callback` is the optional callback method to call to acknowledge the receipt of the event.

Emitting an event

We use the `emit` method to trigger an event. This event will be handled on the server:

```
socket.on(<event>, <event_data>, ack_callback);
```

Here, `event` is the name of the event to trigger, `event_data` is the event data as a JSON object, and `ack_callback` is the optional callback function that is invoked on the successful receipt of the message on the server.

Sending a message

The `send` method is used to send a message to the server:

```
socket.send(<message>, ack_callback);
```

Here, `message` is the message that will be sent to the server and `ack_callback` is the optional callback function that is invoked on the successful receipt of the message on the server.

Client events

In this section we will get to know some client-side events.

connect

The `connect` event is emitted when the socket is connected successfully:

```
socket.on('connect', function () {})
```

connecting

The `connecting` event is emitted when the socket is attempting to connect with the server:

```
socket.on('connecting', function () {})
```

disconnect

The `disconnect` event is emitted when the socket is disconnected:

```
socket.on('disconnect', function () {})
```

connect_failed

The `connect_failed` event is emitted when socket.io fails to establish a connection to the server for reasons such as when none of the transports work or authorization failed:

```
socket.on('connect_failed', function () {})
```

error

The `error` event is emitted when an error occurs and it cannot be handled by the other event types:

```
socket.on('error', function () {})
```

message

The `message` event is emitted when a message sent with `socket.send` is received:

```
socket.on('message', function (<message>, <ack_callback>) {})
```

Here, `message` is the sent message and `ack_callback` is an optional acknowledgment function.

reconnect

The `reconnect` event is emitted when socket.io successfully reconnects to the server:

```
socket.on('reconnect', function () {})
```

reconnecting

The `reconnecting` event is emitted when the socket is attempting to reconnect with the server:

```
socket.on('reconnecting', function () {})
```

reconnect_failed

The `reconnect_failed` event is emitted when socket.io fails to reestablish a working connection after the connection was dropped:

```
socket.on('reconnect_failed', function () {})
```

B
Socket.IO Backends

Socket.io started in Node.js and the primary backend continues to be Node.js. This book focuses on building a chat system with socket.io, Node.js, and Express.js. But what if your primary platform of choice is not Node.js or you are working on a project where you want the same capabilities as provided by socket.io but cannot as you have an existing standardized platform and cannot bring a new system in the equation. Many before you have faced the same dilemma and in the spirit of open source, socket.io servers exist for various platforms. In this appendix let's take a look at the various implementations available for socket.io backends.

Every platform will require you to apply the learning and logic from this book to rewrite the server-side code targeting that platform. The client code can continue to be the same.

The following is an alphabetic list of the implementations by their languages/platforms:

Erlang

There are two different backends for socket.io on erlang, Yurii Rashkovskii's **socket. io-erlang** (https://github.com/yrashk/socket.io-erlang) and Yongboy's **erlang-socketio**(https://code.google.com/p/erlang-scoketio/).

Yurii seems to have a disagreement with the path taken by socket.io's post-0.6.x releases, and so the library supports only up to Version 0.6 of the spec. Naturally, most of the examples in this book and many other examples on the Internet, won't work over it.

Yongboy's erlang-socketio seems to be keeping itself up to date with the latest happenings in socket.io and is compatible with the latest spec for socket.io-1.0 at the time of writing. Thus we will focus the rest of this section on this library.

This library is available for **Cowboy** and **Mochiweb**, two popular server-side frameworks in erlang. Both these versions support socket.io spec 1.0. The Cowboy version supports all the transports, while the Mochiweb version is limited to `xhr-polling`, `htmlfile`, and `json-polling`.

Google Go

Go is a language in its early years, but is gaining popularity, mainly due to the corporate backing from Google and being one of the three languages supported on the Google App Engine, beside Python and Java.

The `go-socket.io` implementation provides socket.io support on Go. This project supports almost all the transports and also supports socket.io on Google's App Engine. The original codebase for this project is at `https://github.com/madari/go-socket.io`, but the development there has stagnated for a while; but others seem to have taken up the torch. The socket.io wiki points to this fork:

`https://github.com/davies/go-socket.io`.

One thing to notice here is that this codebase still doesn't support versions higher than 0.6.x.

Check out the forks created in github and you will find interesting developments being done to the code. Like this fork, which was updated much more recently:

`https://github.com/justinfx/go-socket.io`.

If you want to use a newer version of socket.io, the fork at `https://github.com/murz/go-socket.io` should support versions up to 0.8.x (this was at the time of writing).

Java

There are multiple implementations available for socket.io on a Java server. Let's take a look at them.

The first is **Socket.IO-Java**, maintained most actively at `https://github.com/Ovea/Socket.IO-Java`. It has been forked and modified to work with various servers and platforms.

Then there is **Atmosphere**. Atmosphere began as a project to bring server push to glassfish servers, but was spun off as a project of its own and works with almost any Java server. Atmosphere server comes with atmosphere.js, which is its own JS client, but any Atmosphere application will work with a socket.io client out of the box, without any modification; use `https://github.com/Atmosphere/atmosphere/wiki/Getting-Started-with-Socket.IO` to get started with Atmosphere,. If you are starting a new java project or are introducing push in your existing java one, don't make a decision until you have taken a look at Atmosphere.

Netty brings an asynchronous server to Java; and very important to mention is Yongboy's **socketio-netty** (`http://code.google.com/p/socketio-netty/`). It is highly recommended due to the async nature of netty, which is more suited for these applications.

Gisio (`https://bitbucket.org/c58/gnisio/wiki/Home`) brings socket.io to the GWT framework, the Google's write-in-Java-and-compile-to-JS library. So if your application is built in GWT and you want to introduce server-push in your application, you can use this library.

And for the new and upcoming completely asynchronous server **Vert.x**, there is **mod-socket-io** (`https://github.com/keesun/mod-socket-io`) Again, if you are looking at an application of a highly asynchronous nature, I would suggest you to take a look at this server and this module.

Perl

Perl may be a very old language, but is still used in many places, and it has an actively maintained socket.io server module called **pocketio** (`https://github.com/vti/pocketio`).

Python

Python is another language that is gaining wide acceptance and popularity. And there are multiple socket.io server implementations for Python.

The first we look at is **gevent-socket.io** (`https://github.com/abourget/gevent-socketio`), which works with any WSGI-based web frameworks. So if you are using any framework such as Pyramid, Pylons, Flask, and Django, this will work for you. The only dependencies are **gevent** and **gevent-websocket**.

If Tornado is your framework of choice, take a look at **Tornadio 2** (`https://github.com/MrJoes/tornadio2`), which provides support for socket.io Versions 0.7 and higher. Again, Tornado is an asynchronous framework and good for such applications.

And dedicated to bringing socket.io to Django is **django-socketio** (`https://github.com/stephenmcd/django-socketio`).

Summary

In this chapter we saw the socket.io backend implementations for some popular platforms. If you are using some other platform, just search for a socket.io server implementation on the Internet and I am sure you will find one. It may not be the best or in an ideal state, but you definitely will find a solution to get started.

Index

exit event 104
Express JS 34-42

F

files
  serving 32-34
Forever 100
forever stop command 100

G

gaming 13
get method 112
gevent 119
gevent-socket.io 119
gevent-websocket 119
Gisio 119
Go 118

H

Haml 40
handshake property 85
HAProxy
  defining 101
  working 101, 102
Hello Web 20-22
Hello World with Node.js 20
HTTP methods 27, 28

I

initialize method 53
io.of method 67
io.sockets.on event 52

J

Jade 40
JavaScript 9
join method 112
join_room event 73
jQuery
  adding 48

K

ket.io-Java 118

L

listen method 51

M

message event 116
Mochiweb 118
mod-socket-io 119
modules
  creating 29-32
Monit
  defining 99
  using 100

N

name_set event 85
namespaces
  working with 66-70
Netty 119
node
  executing, tips 107
node cluster 103, 104
Node.js
  about 15
  features 16-18
  obtaining 19
  origin 16
Node.js, features
  corporate backing 18
  event-driven design 17, 18
  JavaScript 16, 17
Node.js package manager (npm) 19

P

Perl 119
Persevere 16
pocketio 119
production environment 97, 98
Python 119

R

real-time web
  about 7, 8
  AJAX Request 10

U

Upstart 101
user_entered event 64
user messages 49
user name
  sharing 81-85
users
  in chat room 63
  name, assigning 57-63

V

V8 16
Vert.x 119

W

web-based monitors 14
WebSocket API 88, 89
WebSocket protocol
  limitations 87, 88
write method 22

Y

yum command 99

Thank you for buying
Socket.IO Real-time Web Application Development

About Packt Publishing

Packt, pronounced 'packed', published its first book *"Mastering phpMyAdmin for Effective MySQL Management"* in April 2004 and subsequently continued to specialize in publishing highly focused books on specific technologies and solutions.

Our books and publications share the experiences of your fellow IT professionals in adapting and customizing today's systems, applications, and frameworks. Our solution based books give you the knowledge and power to customize the software and technologies you're using to get the job done. Packt books are more specific and less general than the IT books you have seen in the past. Our unique business model allows us to bring you more focused information, giving you more of what you need to know, and less of what you don't.

Packt is a modern, yet unique publishing company, which focuses on producing quality, cutting-edge books for communities of developers, administrators, and newbies alike. For more information, please visit our website: www.packtpub.com.

About Packt Open Source

In 2010, Packt launched two new brands, Packt Open Source and Packt Enterprise, in order to continue its focus on specialization. This book is part of the Packt Open Source brand, home to books published on software built around Open Source licenses, and offering information to anybody from advanced developers to budding web designers. The Open Source brand also runs Packt's Open Source Royalty Scheme, by which Packt gives a royalty to each Open Source project about whose software a book is sold.

Writing for Packt

We welcome all inquiries from people who are interested in authoring. Book proposals should be sent to author@packtpub.com. If your book idea is still at an early stage and you would like to discuss it first before writing a formal book proposal, contact us; one of our commissioning editors will get in touch with you.

We're not just looking for published authors; if you have strong technical skills but no writing experience, our experienced editors can help you develop a writing career, or simply get some additional reward for your expertise.

Node Web Development

ISBN: 978-1-849515-14-6   Paperback: 172 pages

A practical introduction to Node, the exciting new server-side JavaScript web development stack

1. Go from nothing to a database-backed web application in no time at all

2. Get started quickly with Node and discover that JavaScript is not just for browsers anymore

3. An introduction to server-side JavaScript with Node, the Connect and Express frameworks, and using SQL or MongoDB database back-end

Node Cookbook

ISBN: 978-1-849517-18-8   Paperback: 342 pages

Over 50 recipes to master the art of asynchronous server-side JavaScript using Node

1. Packed with practical recipes taking you from the basics to extending Node with your own modules

2. Create your own web server to see Node's features in action

3. Work with JSON, XML, web sockets, and make the most of asynchronous programming

Please check **www.PacktPub.com** for information on our titles

Getting Started with Meteor.js JavaScript Framework

Getting Started with Meteor.js JavaScript Framework

Develop modern web applications in Meteor, one of the hottest new JavaScript platforms

Isaac Strack

[PACKT] open source ✳

Getting Started with Meteor.js JavaScript Framework

ISBN: 978-1-782160-82-3   Paperback: 130 pages

Develop modern web applications in Meteor, one of the hottest new JavaScript platforms

1. Create dynamic, multi-user web applications completely in JavaScript

2. Use best practice design patterns including MVC, templates, and data synchronization

3. Create simple, effective user authentication including Facebook and Twitter integration

4. Learn the time-saving techniques of Meteor to code powerful, lightning-fast web apps in minutes

Learning Modernizr

Learning Modernizr

Create forward-compatible websites using feature detection features of Modernizr

Adam Watson

[PACKT] open source ✳

Learning Modernizr

ISBN: 978-1-782160-22-9   Paperback: 118 pages

Create forward-compatible websites using feature detection features of Modernizr

1. Build a progressive experience using a vast array of detected CSS3 features

2. Replace images with CSS based counterparts

3. Learn the benefits of detecting features instead of checking the name and version of the browser and serving accordingly

Please check **www.PacktPub.com** for information on our titles